DOMUNI
A COLLECTIVE ADVENTURE

Fr. Michel VAN AERDE, op

DOMUNI
A COLLECTIVE
1998 - 2023

Domuni-Press

2025

THIS BOOK IS PUBLISHED
BY DOMUNI-PRESS
IN THE
HISTORY COLLECTION

ISSN : 2551-6744
ISBN : 978-2-36648-236-2
© DOMUNI-PRESS, July 2025

The intellectual property code prohibits copies or reproductions intended for collective use. Representation or reproduction in whole or in part by any means whatsoever, without the consent of the author or his successors, is unlawful and constitutes an infringement of copyright under articles L.335-2 and following of the Intellectual Property Code.

www.domuni.eu

To the reader unknown

Thanks to you, in writing this story, I have rediscovered the spring of my first strides. After twenty-five years, the initial enthusiasm had given way to the long-distance runner's fatigue. Calling our forerunners on the phone to listen to their testimonial, reviving my memory, opening the archives, confronting myself with the founding documents, rekindled the enthusiasm of the early days. The many articles, letters exchanged, drawings and photographs bear witness to this.

Domuni's innovation was part of an underlying movement, driven by an unfailing optimism – that of the joyful discovery of a new continent. Without yet having experienced it, everyone was already delighted with the potential of new technologies for teaching. It was within reach, so simple that it already seemed accomplished. We could feel the cultural treasures multiplied by sharing.

This book conveys to you the rumours of a collective adventure that, merely by reading these lines, you are already taking part in. Your place is ready, whether you are a student, teacher or researcher, passionate about shared knowledge, exchanges of truth, reasoning and resonance, insights and syntheses. Your place is ready in this international and intercultural university world.

This book invites you to discover the beginnings: the quiet roots, the improbable encounters, the great turning points when the unexpected happens – a pandemic, new software, the call of faraway islands... In this global village, exotic music, dance steps and liturgies resonate and interweave. The world is small, dizzyingly deep and infinitely diverse.

Reader, perhaps you are already writing the next pages of this shared adventure?

A snapshot of Domuni in 2023

The hiker who reaches the pass, before sitting down on a mossy rock and opening their backpack to eat and drink, turns around. Even before admiring the panoramic view, they pull out their smartphone to send a photo to their friends. They want to convey what they have not yet seen, what they are about to discover, by sharing it as they revel in it. They forget the "Why?" that assailed them when brambles scratched them, when stones rolled under their feet, when the rain washed over them, when their higher steps tested their knees. Here they are, breathing in the landscape, filling their lungs with the space they envision. Paid to do so, they would have refused. Sharing their ascent is their reward. The fact that it is perfectly free, of price and obligation – and perhaps pointless – increases tenfold their pride in sharing it.

In the snapshot, we are at the end of 2023. The baton has just been passed. The first rector to be elected, Marie Monnet, is driving forward a new momentum. Domuni scores 4.8 out of 5 in its Google reviews, and the beneficiaries express – in their own words – a satisfaction that corresponds so precisely to the mission of our school that it could almost be considered suspect:

> *Domuni offers an absolutely fascinating and rewarding philosophy course. I commend the immense quality of the teaching, the ease of access to the faculty's platform, and the availability and unfailing support of the professors. Domuni makes it possible to follow a demanding course of study in parallel with a professional life, thanks to the much appreciated flexibility in the duration of studies. I can only highly recommend this university, whose long experience of distance learning can be felt throughout the course.*

We did it. The challenge has been met! Before crossing the pass for other adventures, we can sit down and take a break.

The inevitable question always comes up: how many students do you have? Before answering, we have to ask ourselves exactly what we are counting. Is it people? Hands? Fingers?

The "student" category is anything but homogenous. Do we include auditors in the same way as those who follow a long academic course – two, three, five, sometimes eight years – with real participation on our platform? But usually, people do not care about these nuances. They want a figure. Clear. Sharp. A single one.

The www.domuni.eu website lists 3,500 students.

The reaction to this figure is instantaneous: *That's a lot!* – with a strong exclamation mark. That *is* a lot of students. And to support these students, 380 teachers are mobilised, offering more than 1,000 courses. Around thirty administrative, technical and teaching staff form the heart of the reactor.

Domuni Universitas comprises three faculties: theology, philosophy, humanities and social sciences. Teaching is offered in five languages: French, English, Italian, Spanish and Arabic. The latter is non-European, giving our offering a unique cross-cultural outlook.

Our teaching is entirely distance learning, which in itself is nothing new. Other establishments have preceded it – and not the least. The CNED (Centre National d'Enseignement à Distance, for National Centre for Distance Learning), founded in 1939, trains over 160,000 students in 182 courses. The Open University (UK), founded in 1965, boasts over 2 million students worldwide.

Today, a wide range of disciplines – law, mathematics, architecture and even theoretical medicine – are taught online. So what makes Domuni so unique? Three words sum it up: flexibility, transdisciplinarity and transculturality.

Flexibility is at the heart of our success. It explains the constant growth in our student numbers, including in disciplines often perceived as less attractive – theology, history or philosophy. For many, this flexibility is decisive: beyond simple geographical freedom, the Internet is redefining our relationship with time. With us, students progress at their own pace, with immediate access to courses, 24 hours a day, wherever they are in the world.

Furthermore, **transdisciplinarity** is rooted in the diversity of our students' professional backgrounds, the majority of whom are aged between 25 and 44. This diversity enriches our exchanges and enriches our teaching. At the same time, our range of cross-disciplinary courses reinforces this approach, by mixing disciplines and broadening the intellectual horizons of each student.

Finally, **transculturality** is self-evident, driven by the geographical diversity of our community of students and teachers. Each exchange is enriched by the variety of cultural contexts, offering a fertile intellectual decentring.

It is significant that the deans and vice-deans of our faculties come from different cultural backgrounds – Africa, Haiti, Oceania, Europe. In a world that is increasingly attentive to intellectual decolonisation, it is essential for a university system to recognise the plurality of cultures. We have achieved this.

To these three fundamental characteristics, we have added a fourth, which runs counter to current trends: **simplicity**. Not through minimalism, but through a conscious choice: a form of pedagogical asceticism and technological sobriety.

Rather than saturating our students' minds with videoconferences, we have chosen the written word as our main medium of transmission. It is the simplest, most precise and most durable method[1].

It is through the written word that philosophy has been passed down through the centuries. It was through the written word that the Bible took shape. The written word makes it possible to revisit difficult concepts and skim over those that have already been mastered. It offers everyone a personalised and autonomous learning experience.

Short videos are used as a complement. They introduce the lessons and set the scene, without requiring excessive note-taking. This

---

[1] There are two reasons for choosing the written word. The first is educational, as we have just explained. The second is social: as connections are often poor, the use of videos excludes the poorest. The initial choice of the written word is a wise one, because the trend has been reversed: on the phone, candidates are reassured when they learn that they will be using written texts as a basis. Who has watched video lessons for more than 30 hours at a time without getting discouraged?

approach allows students to concentrate on the essentials, explore complex subjects in depth, and navigate their study path with ease.

The many unsolicited applications to teach or publish a book with Domuni-Press bear witness to the recognition of our institution. Publications (books and journal articles) are selected by an independent reading committee, which guarantees their scientific quality. A rigorous procedure is also in place for courses. The proposed content is first evaluated by two lecturers specialising in the field concerned, who check that it meets the school's academic standards. Their opinion is then forwarded to the Faculty Council, which decides whether or not to approve the course. The final decision is notified by the General Secretariat. When a course is approved, a contract is signed with the teacher. Additional elements are then added: presentation of the course, teaching objectives, learning outcomes, as well as videos, quizzes, assignments and exams, in accordance with the terms and conditions agreed with the faculty.

Today, our educational heritage includes a thousand courses, a veritable treasure trove of knowledge accessible to all, an intangible asset that is enriched by being shared. Domuni stands out not only for its body of researchers and teachers, but also for the exceptional quality of its educational corpus, as evidenced by the reviews it receives. This digitised content is regularly updated by its authors or the teachers who have taken over from them. They do not start with a blank slate, but enrich and adapt the existing courses instead, by updating the bibliography, the topics and by providing additions.

From the outset, the core courses have been provided in different versions by teachers with complementary perspectives, ensuring an ongoing dialogue between teachers, and between generations.

This perpetuates, in a modern way, the medieval tradition of "readers" and glosses in the margins of parchments, but with a much broader synthesis, facilitated by digitisation.

A pedagogical and technical team provides the impetus for this body of teaching through personalised mentoring. Some teachers combine multiple talents: researchers, writers, teachers and experts in teaching platforms, mastering digital tools to guide students in the development of their thinking. Other specialised teachers can draw on the team's skills to adapt their content for teaching purposes, without having to master complex software.

The treasure trove of teaching content, protected by contracts, is a recognised asset in the institution's accounts. It is the primary source of quality and a guarantee of continuity, more valuable than any building, even a historic one. These lectures, like the unpublished documents accessible through our "online resources", are in a way intellectual historical monuments, saved from oblivion. You can listen to the voice of Brother Marie-Dominique Chenu[2], recounting his journey from the expulsions from France to the Council; read the lectures by Brother Marie Michel Labourdette, Brother François Genuyt and Brother Jacques Jomier; or discover previously unpublished lectures by Brother Jean Michel Maldamé and many other rare gems.

Beyond its originality, how does our institution manage to be so viable, when other renowned establishments that have adopted a similar model have not met with the same success? Does the key lie in choosing entirely distance learning? Other institutions have also opted for this approach. However, perhaps they have not pushed the envelope as we did regarding the organisation of distance learning exams, the flexibility of enrolment dates or the total freedom to work at their own pace?

Some very close partners have adopted our model, going so far as to share the same teaching platform. For example, the Priory Institute has joined us for English, Francesco Compagnoni and his team for Italian, and the Dominican provinces of Spain for Spanish. However, some of them gave up. What did they miss? What are the specifics that have enabled our international team to develop the institution, while others, following separate paths, have run out of steam?

How can we maintain the balance between diversity and unity, coherence and creativity in the future? This book, in the form of a testimonial, offers food for thought and answers to these questions.

Two words sum up our practical approach: accessibility and availability. All our courses are immediately available as soon as

---

[2] www.domuni.eu/fr/recherche/les-ressources-en-ligne/audio/37/interview-de-m-d-chenu-37.

students log on to their study plan on DoMoodle[3], our teaching platform, using their login details. Each theory course is accessible in full, and students progress at their own pace, working through the modules one after the other. Students interact with teachers through course forums and benefit from personalised support, encouraged and guided by a mentor, a doctor in the field, rather than a simple assistant as is the case elsewhere.

Too good to be true? The testimonials confirm *the availability and unfailing support of the teachers.*

Our mountain hiking metaphor needs to be fleshed out more. Instead of setting off equipped with everything we needed to see us through – good shoes, provisions and water – we took the first step empty-handed, without a pack or a stick. "We", because I was not alone: not only did we have to move forward, but we also had to train troops – troops that first had to be recruited, a double challenge. The gamble, or rather the faith, consisted in "acting as if" the resources were going to present themselves, as and when they were needed. So it was all about taking the first step, without thinking about the disproportion between available resources and future needs, without thinking about the problems that would arise, without thinking about the obstacles that would arise: that simple first step that would have to be multiplied, added up...

The history of Domuni has not been that of a hiking trail mapped out in advance. No GPS, but the Holy Spirit, who never turned us away. Our best guess was to head for the hidden paths, far from the honking herd of saturated motorways. Where were we going? Knowing too soon would have made us lose heart. Only one thing was certain: we were heading somewhere else, somewhere different.

How shall this be?[4] Caution is a virtue that I appreciate as long as it does not put the brakes on a project prematurely. *Abraham set out... without knowing where he was going!* It is the first impulse that counts, an impulse, almost a folly, that qualifies everything else along the way. Charity is an urge, one that implies sharing our knowledge[5].

---

[3] Since 2025, this platform has been called MyDomuni.
[4] Lk 1:34.
[5] "*...a specific form of charity: intellectual charity,*" Pope Francis often repeats.

Hope communicates confidence, and faith therefore remains unwavering.

The photo shows where we started from; i.e., from the bottom, from nothing, not one student, not one course, not one penny: ground zero. Paradoxical maxims enlightened us along the way. *The call is only heard in the response itself*[6]. *The fire proves the spark that started it*[7]. *They did not know it was impossible, that is why they did it*[8]!

In 2005, Guido Van Damme, a lay Dominican and former editor-in-chief of the Belgian daily *Le Soir*, told me: *a newspaper is a reader, plus a reader, plus a reader*. I used to translate it this way: one student, plus one student, plus one student. Or a course, plus a course..., a curriculum, plus a curriculum..., a language, plus a language, plus another language. The path, now contemplated with a single glance, has in fact been discovered step by step, or more precisely invented turn by turn, pass by pass, ford by ford. It was renewed storm after storm, welcome after welcome, support after support, friendship after friendship, joy after joy. There was no map, no five-year plan; nothing was written in advance, just a course to follow, towards which even the headwinds made us progress.

Failure is the father of the next success, and if it were easy, everyone would do it, I often said to my colleagues, as much to encourage them as to reassure myself. Some people pointed out that I had the stubbornness of a bull. I did not believe in the signs of the zodiac, but I was determined. I would go for it all, and if in doubt, I would go for it. Would I have done it without faith? This was not even a question. Faith in the resurrection of the just crucified is faith in a God who is master of the impossible.

Paradoxically, we were lucky enough to develop our teaching methods before the advent of video-conferencing tools to facilitate synchronous teaching. If, from the outset, we had had technologies

---

[6] Emmanuel Levinas.

[7] Roger Garaudy.

[8] Attributed to Mark Twain, British Prime Minister Winston Churchill, or even US President J.F. Kennedy, but actually from Marcel Pagnol, since it appears on page 145 of the third volume of his *Œuvres complètes ("Complete Works", Cinématurgie de Paris, César, Merlusse)*, published in 1967.

that offered a quality close to that of face-to-face teaching, we would probably have neglected asynchronous organisation. And yet, although more complex to set up, it is this approach that has enabled us to achieve the essential: accessibility.

Let us be clear. Today's technologies almost make it possible to match the quality of remote face-to-face sessions, to the point where the notion of synchronous is tending to replace that of face-to-face. However, synchronisation concerns time, not place. So it is no longer a question of rethinking space, but of rethinking time management. The question of space is resolved by distance learning, which in turn makes it possible to create a more flexible relationship with time through an asynchronous system. This flexibility in terms of time is decisive because it means that those with rigid agendas can be accommodated.

What the advocates of blended learning[9] fail to grasp is that 100% asynchronous teaching meets the needs of a large and specific audience: people who already work.

It is this major shift that explains why our institution has always refused to give up on 100% remote access, despite fashions and adverse pressures. By force of circumstance, we have found ourselves in a quasi-monopolistic position, without having sought it.

The university context

Students face many constraints: location, timetable, resources. Universities, for their part, have their own limitations: intake capacity, teaching staff, administration and budget. Today, the tension between supply and demand is palpable, with growing training needs on the one hand, and university intake capacity struggling to keep pace on the other. On the front page of Le Monde on 12 May 2024, we read *Des universités au bord de l'asphyxie* (Universities on the verge of suffocation).

The current situation in some areas, such as medical education, borders on the unimaginable. For years, the shortage of doctors has

---

[9] Blended: distance and face-to-face.

been pushing French students to go abroad (Belgium, Romania, etc.) to get round the strict selection process in the first year. A new stage was reached when a town like Orléans invited its students to enrol by distance learning at the University of Zagreb, in Croatia[10], in response to this shortage.

In addition, under the impetus of the University of Toulouse, French law faculties have set up distance learning programmes. Costs, which were €2,000 in 2005, have risen to around €6,000 ten years later: and as students can keep working, they are able to finance their training.

> **Cost per student for the French state**
>
> For the French state, the cost of a student varies from €10,000 a year at university to €16,000 for a student in a preparatory class for the grandes écoles. These costs will continue to rise for face-to-face courses, whereas distance learning can reduce them considerably. Our school offers annual enrolments at a cost six times lower than that borne by the State for each university student. Furthermore, with so many bursaries on offer, even the Ministry of Finance recognises that we offer a not-for-profit service of general interest[11].
>
> We have compared tuition fees and costs per student per academic year, with the ultimate aim of graduating. Efficiency is an essential criterion. For the State, a successful degree costs **€77,300**; for Domuni, the cost to the State is zero. For Domuni, the calculation is $3 \times 1{,}800 \times 100/80 = $ **€6,750**, which is more than ten times more productive than the public education system.

---

[10] "Faire ses études de médecine en Roumanie : Il n'y a pas cette concurrence avec les autres étudiants" (Studying medicine in Romania: There is no competition with other students), *L'Étudiant*, 2 May 2023. [Online]. "In September 2022, the City of Orléans and the *Medical Studies in English* international medical school in Zagreb (Croatia) entered into a partnership to train medical students. [...]. During the years of training prior to residency, the city of Orléans and the Loiret department offer grants to students who undertake, under contract, to practise for at least five years in Orléans or the Loiret region, once they have completed their studies and obtained their doctorate [...]. As a reminder, the MSE Zagreb diploma is recognised in France under a 2013 European directive" [orleans-metropole.fr, "Ouverture des inscriptions pour la faculté publique internationale de médecine de Zagreb, la *Medical Studies in English*" (Registration opens for Zagreb's international public medical school, *Medical Studies in English*)]. See also "Le vice-doyen de la faculté de médecine de Zagreb s'explique sur son projet de partenariat avec Orléans" (The vice-dean of Zagreb's Faculty of Medicine explains his partnership project with Orléans), *France Bleu*, 21 February 2022. [Online].

[11] Document dated 28 January 2014.

Competition is now international, and to face up to it, it is strategic to benefit from certain protected niches. Our school has developed in the French language, which is a less competitive sector than English. Teaching began with theology, supported by the Dominican label, a guarantee of quality. Other disciplines, often neglected by national universities, are also areas in which our institution legitimises its expertise: philosophy, history, art history and human rights, areas in which the Order of Preachers has a long history of commitment. On the other hand, fields such as administration, economics, marketing and management are particularly competitive areas, dominated by the business schools, which are waging a fierce battle.

However, as a continuation of *Économie et Humanisme* (Economy and Humanism), founded by Brother Joseph Lebret, O.P., our institution, in partnership with actors in disadvantaged countries, promotes an equitable economy.

As for the exact sciences, they require technical resources beyond our reach, and are not part of the Order's tradition – however much we may think of Albertus Magnus. On the other hand, in 2024, our institution will be the only one to offer online degree courses in Arabic, for bachelors and masters degrees in Christian theology, as well as a master's degree in religious studies. Collaboration with our partners should enable us to extend this offer to other disciplines in the future.

There are four challenges facing universities in the 21st century: climate change, migration, rapid population growth and exponentially rising costs. A university like Strasbourg stopped heating its buildings for more than a month in the winter of 2024, extending its holidays and switching to full distance learning as part of an "energy saving" programme.

What role can universities play in the migration phenomenon? It may not be very visible, but it is very important. When hope for oneself and one's family collapses, migration becomes the only option, despite the risks and costs. However, thanks to online training and teleworking, hope can be rekindled. Connection breaks down isolation, and in this "global village", notions of relocation or migration lose their meaning. People can study and work from anywhere, without having to leave their homes or countries of origin.

Domuni strives to promote social justice by adopting an economic model that avoids restricting access to university to the financial elite. Thanks to affordable tuition fees and a generous system of scholarships, our institution gives disadvantaged people access to higher education, particularly in poor countries that are often neglected.

Non-European students, including those from disadvantaged regions, have to pay tuition fees that are often five times higher than in Belgium or the UK, a paradoxical and unfair situation.

Forty per cent of English universities are in deficit. Faced with stagnating local tuition fees since 2017 (£9,250 a year), they have sought to attract more international students, for whom fees are much higher (up to £67,000 a year at Cambridge for medicine). Income from international students rose from £5.4 billion to £9.7 billion between 2016 and 2022. This rise changed the make-up of universities, with a significant increase in Indian and Nigerian students, replacing Europeans affected by Brexit. However, this trend came to an abrupt halt in 2024, due to new government restrictions aimed at limiting immigration, banning foreign students from coming with their families.

Accreditations are never definitive[12]. They have to be renewed periodically, even for national universities. Will Europe one day develop a supranational system for this? A university can hold several accreditations, as can any consortium of universities to which it may belong.

Our institution is already working with various universities (Tangaza University, UAC, UNSTA, UNDH, Angelicum, UCLouvain, University of Lorraine, ICES, etc.) to offer joint courses. Our higher education institution was originally conceived as a university consortium, so it is familiar with offering courses that are the result of pooling the academic resources of several universities.

---

[12] Unesco, "Global Convention on the Recognition of Qualifications concerning Higher Education", Paris, 2019.

This pooling enables us to guarantee excellent training by selecting the best teachers in each region. Furthermore, it makes it possible to intervene in strategic locations, avoiding being limited to a purely theoretical or bibliographical universe. Thanks to this network, we are in a position to offer training tailored to the specific needs of disadvantaged areas, by training people capable of working directly in the field, in particular during internships in real-life conditions. This is part of the dynamic promoted by the Master of the Order through the University Network of the Order of Preachers (UNOP), which is made up of Dominican universities.

When we started teaching remotely, the first objection was that e-learning was impractical. Then, critics focused on quality. Once quality became indisputable, objections focused on the validity of diplomas and accreditation. At the same time, legislation evolved. Under international pressure, the French state incorporated the term "accreditation" into its vocabulary and, in 2016, adopted the Law for a Digital Republic[13], stipulating that all training, whether distance or face-to-face, is equivalent, as are the resulting diplomas.

Who recognises whom? The central element is trust: that of the students who enrol and that of their future employers. This trust is measured by the growing number of students, the positions they are offered and their career advancement. Ultimately, it is the employers who, by judging the skills of the graduates, validate the quality of the training received.

On 20 April 2024, Catherine Vautrin, the French Minister for Health, published an article in Le Monde entitled: "Pour en finir avec le dogme du diplôme d'État" (Ending the dogma of the state diploma). When needs become pressing, monopolies end up being called into question.

Universities have been in crisis for a long time, and student absenteeism has steadily worsened over the last 60 years. A genuine effort of reflection is needed, refocusing on the primary mission of universities: the transmission of knowledge to students.

---

[13] Law no. 2016-1321 of 7 October 2016 for a Digital Republic, available online at Légifrance.

In his document *Veritatis Gaudium*[14], Pope Francis speaks of a "cultural revolution" and calls for a radical paradigm shift. Nothing less!

> *This daunting task, which cannot be postponed, requires, at the cultural level of university education and scientific research, a generous and convergent commitment to **a radical change of paradigm**, and even – if I may add – to a "brave cultural revolution". In this commitment, the worldwide network of universities and ecclesiastical faculties is called upon to make the decisive contribution of the leaven, salt and light of the Gospel of Jesus Christ and of the living Tradition of the Church, always open to new scenarios and new proposals. (*Pope Francis, *Veritatis Gaudium no. 4)*

What social service do we provide? To understand our institution, it is essential to go back to its origins, an alternative and atypical project in technological, organisational and economic terms. In the early days, there were no financial resources, and there was no need for them. It all started on a voluntary basis, with a shared desire to create a different model.

On the teaching side, the teachers began by offering the content of their courses free of charge. And not just any teachers: the best ones, those who had confidence in their expertise and were not afraid to open up their teaching to everyone. They had often devoted a large part of their lives to this work, writing books and carrying out in-depth research. I could mention a few names, although the list is long: the Dominican brothers Jean-Michel Maldamé, Jacques Jomier, Jean-Marie Mérigoux, Philippe Lefebvre, Jean-Christophe de Nadaï, Bernard Quelquejeu..., and many others from outside the Order, such as Fathers Anselme Baudelet (Benedictine), Luc Brésard, Irénée Rigolo, Augustin Tavardon (Trappist), or Father Bruno Callebaut (diocesan).

The General Chapter of Bologna, which had encouraged the creation of Domuni even before it was officially named, had asked the brothers to contribute by teaching. The response was generous: those who were teaching saw this as an opportunity to disseminate their research internationally. Among them were brothers such as

---

[14] Pope Francis, "Apostolic Constitution *Veritatis Gaudium* on universities and ecclesiastical faculties", *Veritatis Gaudium* no. 4, 29 January 2018.

Ameer Jajé, Serge Thomas Bonino, Gilbert Narcisse, Augustin Laffay, Luc-Thomas Somme, Thierry-Marie Hamonic, Benoît-Dominique de La Soujeole, Jean-Paul Durand, Jean-Miguel Garrigues and Jorel François, as well as Dominican sisters such as Véronique Margron, Marie-Ancilla Durliat, Marie-Louise Lamau and Claire Rousseau, and a Benedictine sister, Sister Véronique Dupont. Deacons such as Jean-Baptiste Echivard and Jacques Fournier, and lay people such as Dominique Lambert, Emmanuel Boissieu and Guy Laurence also answered the call.

The first set the example, and many others followed, placing their trust in our young institution. No one could have disputed the exceptional quality of these lessons.

On the organisational side, Françoise Dubost spent years bringing together a team of young retired university lecturers closely associated with the convent in Toulouse, to digitise the courses, correct spelling mistakes and structure the teaching content before putting it online using the rudimentary IT tools of the time. Michèle Pourteau enriched the courses with "questions to go further", while Hervé Dubost, with Alain Cabanis, managed the accounting. At the time, we were dreaming of achieving 70 enrolments a year. It was a contagious enthusiasm, a thirst for learning and a better understanding of one's faith. Many lay friends happily joined this promising adventure. Theology students experienced a form of happy "disinterestedness" with regard to ecclesiastical diplomas: study was motivated by the quest for truth, research for research's sake. Administration, on the other hand, was still in its infancy.

Years later, our institution has retained this same dynamic, with students, teachers and members of the administration based in regions marked by poverty and conflict, such as Israel, Lebanon, the DRC, Iraq and South Africa. For example, the economics and management course is supervised by Father Wilguens Saint-Fleur, who lives in Haiti, a country where anarchy reigns. The philosophy faculty is run by brother Augustin Wiliwoli, provincial of the Dominicans in the DRC, who defended his thesis at Louvain on conflict resolution, a subject that is sadly relevant in the Congo. Art history is led by Jean-Louis Meylan, who works in Lausanne. The Dean of Social Sciences, Brother Manuel Rivero, a Spaniard, lives in

Saint-Denis de La Réunion and teaches regularly in Madagascar at the Catholic University (UCM). He is also a prison chaplain and holds two doctorates, in communications and theology. The Faculty of Theology is headed by a woman, Sister Évelyne Maurice, who is based in Switzerland.

To fulfil a mission, you have to be in tune with the reality on the ground!

Our institution functions like a living organism, constantly evolving and adapting to meet the demands of quality education. This quality must be present at every stage, from the moment a potential student registers to the moment they obtain a degree, and, for courses, from the submission of a manuscript to the payment of royalties. It is evaluated on an ongoing basis, through surveys completed by students at the end of each course, questionnaires sent out at the end of each course, and indicators that we analyse, such as the average time taken to correct assignments.

The feedback is then passed on to the people in charge, whether teachers or members of the various departments. They can respond to criticism and fix any malfunctions. In the event of serious failings or persistent refusal to listen to feedback, sanctions may be considered, up to and including exclusion from the teaching staff. The quality management system promotes continuous improvement, like a rack-and-pinion train that moves forward with no room for regression.

Domuni, a theology school

Our school was not set up simply to be yet another university, even one at a distance. The aim was to offer an opportunity to those who had no access to higher education.

This objective was intended to be inclusive: a university for all. Inclusivity was not just a matter for students, but also for teachers, whether they were already working elsewhere or were away from teaching centres for various reasons. Thanks to cyberspace, they could join in our efforts to transmit knowledge. Since our institution originated in a Latin American context, it is worth recalling its spiritual and social elements.

A faith that liberates

The term theology seems ill-suited to describe liberation theology, because this movement is first and foremost a practice, before being a theory. Is this enough to dissociate it from classical theology? During a discussion with a person in charge of training young Dominicans, who was sceptical about liberation theology, I asked the question: *Is jazz music?* His answer was cautious: *You cannot say it is just noise.* I then added: *Liberation theology is to classical theology what jazz is to music.* The debate is about practice, about God's involvement in social reality, seen from the perspective of the excluded.

The Haitian Dominican students trained by the Jesuits in Santo Domingo were not asking questions about the Platonic system, but about an existential question: why did Socrates die?

For my interlocutor, this question, raised by a Jesuit teacher who was later murdered, was not philosophical and did not prepare for the study of theology. Perhaps he was not wrong, if you put it in the context of Toulouse, where there was no threat to life. In Haiti or El Salvador, the reality was quite different, and this difference also shed light on fundamental theological questions, such as why Jesus died.

The abstract theology of Jesus of Nazareth did not really differ from that of the doctors of the Law, the scribes and the Pharisees. But he associated God with the integration of public sinners, transgressed the Law by touching lepers, the blind, women and the dying, and relativised the importance of the Temple and the rites.

Similarly, St Paul's theology changed fundamentally after his conversion. When he asked on the road to Damascus: *Who are you, Lord?* The answer is astounding: *I am Jesus whom thou persecutest.*

The biblical God is the one who, throughout the history of Israel, makes an alliance with the oppressed, not because they are better, but precisely because they are oppressed. God takes the initiative to free his people from slavery in Egypt. The story of the Exodus does not hide the difficulties: the liberation took 70 years, and none of those who left Egypt survived to enter the Promised Land. Yet this promise of liberation gives meaning to those whose future is blocked. It has resonated down the centuries, as evidenced by the songs of the black slaves in the cotton fields: *Go down Moses... Let my people go!*

The oppressed, those who have no future, open up history for everyone, because the living God is the God of the impossible, the God who overturns the obvious and calls us to hope.

By avoiding simply reproducing the privileged and getting closer to the field, our institution has had to innovate. Teaching content has been enriched by the experience of people involved in "real" contexts, at the heart of real life, and not just in academic circles. Pedagogy has been transformed, and the impact of research has been strengthened thanks to free online distribution, going beyond the limits of the traditional university setting.

From the poor and for the poor: with limited resources, we had to look for simplicity. The written word was chosen as the main medium. This movement required a technical, administrative and pedagogical structure adapted to disadvantaged people and, by extension, to everyone.

Flexibility in terms of time management has meant that we can cater for a different audience from that of traditional institutions: people with restricted working hours, who are the most numerous. Thanks to them, financial autonomy has been achieved, guaranteeing our freedom. The fundamental principle of liberation theology, according to which the opening up of history and the paths to the future for all depend on a commitment to the weakest, has been confirmed.

It is true that we have encountered resistance, similar to that which the Hebrews faced on their path to liberation. These obstacles, most often internal, took different forms, and we had to be strategic to prevent the project from being nipped in the bud. Paradoxically, the lack of visibility (no physical buildings, no geographical base) proved to be protective.

By committing ourselves to an innovative medium, we had the exhilarating experience of being the messenger, the medium and the message itself. Régis Burnet has brilliantly explored this idea by comparing Saint Paul[15] and McLuhan, going so far as to say that the medium and the message become the reader, or the listener[16].

A university in its infancy, subject to administrative hassles and criticism in bad faith, with internal temptations to advocate elitist "excellence", welcoming teachers of good will, and using an Internet still in its infancy, reflected the weakness of the God announced.

In the same way, the "online" proposal was in keeping with the discreet universality of the resurrection. The renunciation of prestige and the self-effacement of teachers were an integral part of what they were transmitting, *without resorting to the wisdom of discourse, so as not to reduce the cross of Christ to nothing.*

In his article, Régis Burnet highlights a truth that we might not have realised ourselves: *the weakness of the message and the object of the message are matched by the weakness of the messenger, whose very weakness acts as proof. The message is indeed "the messenger".* The criticisms we received about the weakness of our institution in its early days, as well as those about the condition of our students, turned into praise:

> *Paul does not hesitate to say that "the message" is also "the listener". "Consider, brethren, who you are who have received the call of God: there are not among you many who are wise in the eyes of men, nor many who are mighty, nor many who are of good family. But God chose the foolish things of the world to shame the wise; God chose the weak things of the world to shame the strong[17].*

---

[15] "Bonjour l'Ancêtre ! Saint Paul" (Hello Ancestor! Saint Paul), Régis Burnet's article on *Academia*, July 2024, helps us fully grasp what we, in our small way, have experienced: *The particularity of Pauline communication is that it tends to confuse message, messenger and medium. Paul would certainly have laughed at McLuhan's triumphant declaration, which he had invented long ago. He goes much further than asserting that the medium is part of the message: he further asserts that the message is also the messenger, the listener, and that all this is Christ. Indeed, the cardinal term in the apostle's thinking is the gospel, which, as we all know, means good news. But this good news is not just content, it is also personified: in Jesus Christ, whose appearance profoundly changes the messenger, the message, the listener, the world...*

[16] *The medium is the message, the message is the medium, the medium and the message are the messenger, the medium and the message are the listener.*

[17] 1 Corinthians 1:26-27.

The proof of God's strength is not only the weakness of the message, the weakness of Christ, but also the weakness of his listeners. Medium, messenger, message, listener, all combine in a single expression: weakness revealed as strength. [...] the Church is the place where the Gospel is lived and realised, and this realisation is called fraternity. [...] the Pauline Church is above all a networked fraternity[18].

The early days of distance learning gave us the opportunity to experience this uncomfortable but highly motivating process. Today, after sustained development, the spiritual experience continues in other areas, such as that of fraternity and the "network".

When theologians venture into the real problems of life and, out of compassion, take into account the concrete concerns of men and women, they are going off the beaten track. This leads them into dialogue with other disciplines and with non-academic practical knowledge. It is in this transdisciplinarity that theology finds its true dimension, its legitimacy, its social role and its vocation.

How has our team lived through this experience? By responding favourably to several simultaneous calls. Father Wilguens Saint-Fleur, a master's student in theology at Domuni and vice-rector of the Université Notre-Dame d'Haïti (UNDH), asked us to collaborate on MBA master's programmes. At the same time, Father Willy Kibanda, Rector of the University of the Assumption in Congo (UAC), has asked us to work with him on doctoral students in communications.

At the same time, Ms Laetitia de Boeck, winner of the 2016 "Woman of Peace" award, turned to us to organise affordable training courses for economics and management technicians. In addition, volunteer teachers from Haiti, North Africa and sub-Saharan Africa have expressed their desire to contribute to this mission.

By responding creatively to these calls and finding solutions to give them shape, we have had a spiritual experience comparable to that of the multiplication of the loaves. When the poor made their modest contributions (five courses and two seminars, like the five

---

[18] Régis Burnet, *op. cit.*

loaves and two fishes), the needs were met, and even surpassed: a passage from precariousness to abundance, a sign of God's presence.

It was from this experience that the inter-university synergy project was born: pooling courses between several universities to offer together courses that each one could not offer on its own.

In Appendix 1, Sister Marie Monnet talks about an *implicit theology of the Internet*, which is being experienced at Domuni in the context of university life. In his letter to the Ephesians (1:9-10), Saint Paul speaks of a general recapitulation.

> *He made known to us the mystery of His will according to His good pleasure, which He purposed in Christ, to be put into effect when the times reach their fulfillment – to bring unity to all things in heaven and on earth under Christ.*

The recapitulation of knowledge and the density of communication are in harmony, in consonance with Saint Paul's vision of the fulfilment of the universe and of history. There is an analogy here, one of the signs of the times, which enables us to understand what is happening spiritually at another level.

This recapitulation invites us to revisit our relationship with space and time, which we can perceive differently by comparing our experience with the contributions of philosophy and theology.

For the Jews, described by A. Heschel as the *builders of time*, the latter escapes the cycles of "eternal return". It has a meaning, a meaning that does not depend solely on human action, because history is carried by the promise of a "liberating" God. This God, gradually revealed as the "true" and ultimately the "only" God, gives history its eschatological dimension. This messianic perspective became secularised in the 19th century with the utopias of progress, fascism and communism. The bitter failures of atheistic humanism led to post-modernism, which can be overcome by the realisation that, while humanity is incapable of saving itself, someone is taking on the full weight of this mission to bring it to a successful conclusion, whatever the cost.

And so, for Christians, *the* promise has been fulfilled: the Messiah has come and risen, ascended to the highest heaven, so that there is now a centre of time. *He has come, he will come again*, says an Advent preface. Between these two parousias, the resurrection *constitutes the messianic kairos, not as the end of time, but as the very paradigm of the present, of all the present*[19]. In the Christian faith, this "centre of time" is present in all times and gradually recapitulates them, as Saint Paul writes: *He made known to us the mystery of His will according to His good pleasure, which He purposed in Christ, to be put into effect when the times reach their fulfillment – to bring unity to all things in heaven and on earth under Christ*[20].

Our experience of the convergence of knowledge on the Internet helps us to perceive this great mystery. The Jesuit scientist and theologian Teilhard de Chardin[21] distinguished "critical thresholds" in the evolution of the world, corresponding to a succession of windings in the concentration of information: chemical evolution (from atoms to complex molecules), biological life (reproduction and chromosomal memory), conscious life (knowing what we know), and social life (sharing knowledge).

In continuation, the Internet represents a major turning point, in the same way as writing, printing, radio and television. This turning point is marked by the scale of the information available, the immediacy of access, and the organisation of this information via search engines. This process culminates today with AI, which provides organised information, and even better, verbalised information. This impersonal word summarises an immense amount of knowledge in a coherent way.

Although remote, the analogy with theology is enlightening: *the parousia split in this way is understood as a continuous parousia, within this world and based on the initiatives of the new man who would bear witness through his actions to the event that has indeed taken place, but not once and for all: once for all*[22].

The experience of cyberspace is inclusive: "For all", a fundamental principle, as much for the Internet as for the Christian

---

[19] Nathalie Frogneux "Une traversée contemporaine de Paul" (A contemporary crossing of Paul), *Revue d'éthique et de théologie morale*, 2009/3 n° 255, Éditions du Cerf, pp. 63-99.

[20] Ephesians 1:9-10.

[21] See Appendix 4 for an article in the journal *Noosphère*.

[22] Nathalie Frogneux, *op. cit.*

experience, since "Catholic" implies universal. How can we apply this "for all" principle? By reversing the logic of selection, by abandoning the notion of "excellence" (a word that begins with "exclusion"), which consists of wanting to "rise above", "distinguish oneself" or "surpass oneself". Rather than selecting the best, as in the animal world, "for all" places the weakest at the centre of priorities[23], because God identifies with them[24], and calls us to include those who are excluded[25]. Since its inception, this has been the objective of our school, which directs its teaching towards inclusion in higher education[26].

The Dominican tradition insists on *apostolic itinerancy*: moving to reach those to whom the Gospel must be proclaimed. This fluid mobility finds support in convents and monasteries, conceived as stopping-off points rather than centripetal places. Pope Francis often speaks of this, calling for a "Church on the move", a missionary nomadism, as Saint Paul lived it. Today, this means reaching people where they are: on the Internet, especially young people, who are often the most neglected in the transmission of the Gospel. Learning how to make ourselves visible on Google, using social networks, distributing newsletters, creating YouTube channels – these are all ongoing efforts that must be adapted to new media and technologies, and must be carried out in collaboration with those we seek to reach.

---

[23] Mt 23:11: *The greatest among you will be your servant.*

[24] Mk 9:36: *And He took a child and set him in the midst of them. And when He had taken him in His arms, He said unto them, "Whosoever shall receive one of such children in My name, receiveth Me; and whosoever shall receive Me, receiveth not Me, but Him that sent Me." "*

[25] Anthropologists seem to have shown that humanisation coincided with the care of disabled people, unable to live on their own, who mobilised the group and thus constituted it. Prehistoric human burials are evidence of this. See also the concept of the "reversive effect of evolution" by the philosopher Patrick Tort, *Darwin et le Darwinisme* (Darwin and Darwinism), PUF, 1997. 4th ed. 2013. "Natural selection, the guiding principle of evolution, which implies the elimination of the least fit in the struggle for existence, selects a form of social life in humanity whose progress towards 'civilisation' tends to exclude more and more eliminatory behaviour, through the interplay of morality and institutions. In simplified terms, natural selection selects civilisation, which opposes natural selection".

[26] In the same spirit, Jean Vilar spoke of "the elite for all", setting up high-quality productions while aiming to make shows accessible, in terms of price and time, to all audiences. This was part of his wider project to democratise culture.

The heart of time is also the heart of space, accessible through our body, temple of the Spirit and member of the Body of Christ, which is itself the Centre of every place, just as the resurrection is the heart of all time.

> *The body as the place where being and time are knotted [...], because this history is generated in a body, in the most physical and precarious of human bodies, in a body that is also offered, at the same time, to the speaking passage of God*[27].

The intuition of philosophers and theologians, which I quote here, resonates with our experience of teaching remotely: space no longer separates, and, in the asynchronous, time is metamorphosed. In the communion of saints, we are all contemporaries, the only thing that matters is our vigilance, the relational attention that keeps us awake: *The waking have one common world, but the sleeping turn aside each into a world of their own*[28].

> *The body opens the way to the properly Pauline form of transcendence: inclusion as being in Christ. But to do this, we need to read the much-quoted verse from Galatians 3:28 in full: "There is neither Jew nor Greek, there is neither bond nor free, there is neither male nor female; for ye are all one in Christ Jesus". This single sentence contains two Pauline formulas for the universal: the denial of particularism and ethnicity on the one hand, and the universal of inclusion on the other*[29].

Particularisms are not rejected, but transcended. We remain men or women, Jews or not, circumcised Jews or not, it is just that it no longer has the importance we used to attribute to it. Everyone has the right to speak in their own language.

In an ever-renewed Pentecost, particularisms no longer function as exclusions: all particularities are welcome as so many shades of colour and accents, spices and condiments, rhythms and music. The world is celebrating *to bring the times to their fullness* in an immense recapitulation.

---

[27] Bernard Sichère, *Le Jour est proche* (The Day is Close), p. 86, quoted by N. Frogneux, *op. cit.* p. 91.

[28] Heraclitus, fragment 89.

[29] N. Frogneux, *op. cit.* p. 92

Thus, in our principles of action and our experience, an implicit theology emerges, appearing in the language, pedagogy, organisation and very development of our institution. This book seeks to make this theology explicit throughout its pages.

> **Questioning our practice**
>
> Why is the international dimension of teaching so important? Why try to reach people who are excluded from university teaching due to geographical distance, scheduling constraints, or methodological difficulties? And why include teachers with practical experience who are not necessarily in full-time employment? What is the basis for this insistence on inclusion?
>
> Why prioritise democratic governance? What is the basis for this insistence on fraternity?
>
> Why take the risk of engaging with other cultures, traditions and religions? What motivates this attraction to otherness, and what underpins this interest? Why is the written word chosen as the main vehicle for transmitting knowledge while promoting dialogue and contradictory exchange?
>
> Why is there such an interest in new technologies and curiosity about what is new: simply because they are new? Is it because they perform better? Does this attraction to technological progress conceal a form of modernism or progressivism to the detriment of tradition, identity, and fidelity to fundamentals? Can these different trends, which are often perceived as opposites, be reconciled? Can creativity exist without roots? Conversely, does not tradition imply a succession of inspired innovations? Can a balanced tension be maintained between tradition and modernity? Does Domuni have an implicit theology of history?
>
> What is the significance of its claim to belong to the Order of Preachers, and of its rootedness in the Dominican mission? Must managers be exclusively Dominican? Should the majority of teachers be Dominican? What about those who are not?

We have discussed the sources and context of the creation of our institution. It is a spirituality marked by universality and inclusion, and therefore otherness. Dialogue and a concern for transmission clearly emerge. As M.D. Chenu points out, can this spiritual experience be expressed in theological terms?

Theological systems are simply expressions of spirituality. [...] Theology is a spirituality or religious experience that has found an intellectual expression. [...] We do not enter into a system for the logical coherence of its construction or the plausibility of its conclusions; rather, we find ourselves there as if by birth, through the master intuition on which our spiritual life is based, along with the system of intelligibility that this entails. A theology worthy of the name is a spirituality that has found rational instruments adequate to its religious experience. It was no coincidence that Saint Thomas entered the Order of Saint Dominic, nor was it an incoherent grace that the Order of Saint Dominic received Saint Thomas Aquinas. Institution and doctrine are closely linked[30].

Domuni's experience is still developing. By adopting a phenomenological approach and examining our educational model as it evolves, we are exploring the theology that underpins our mission. Debate lies at the heart of our pedagogy, recalling the long Dominican tradition of theological discussion, or *disputatio*.

From the earliest days of the Order of Preachers, theology has always been practised through intellectual exchange, as St Thomas Aquinas demonstrated. He spent his days walking and talking, engaging in public discussions in villages, from Paris to Milan by way of Lyon. Ultimately, his *Summa Theologica* is a vast series of micro-discussions organised into a coherent whole, where the written word follows the spoken word in the form of questions.

St Thomas also set an example of collective work and speed. It is said that he dictated to several secretaries simultaneously, sometimes wearing out three in a day, and that his abbreviated writing was so fast as to be almost reminiscent of modern-day text messages or tweets. He would have been impressed by the speed and efficiency of the internet today.

He did not see his secretaries as mere scribes, but as partners of thought, foreshadowing what we now call "collective intelligence".

---

[30] Marie-Dominique Chenu, O.P., *Une École de Théologie: Le Saulchoir* (A School of Theology: Le Saulchoir), Paris, 1937, p. 75). The reference to Le Saulchoir can shed light on many aspects. See the articles by Brother Henry Donneaud and the books by Étienne Fouilloux for more information.

This collaborative process resembles the modern use of technology and networks to share and co-construct knowledge, which is what Domuni is striving to achieve through its distance learning model.

This method of transmission relies heavily on the written word. Although the written word has become an integral part of our teaching methods, it has not replaced the spoken word. Rather, it is an extension of the spoken word, honouring and extending intellectual debate. In St Thomas' time, the written word naturally followed the spoken word, structuring thought in the form of questions and answers – a process that we find again in quizzes, discussion forums, homework and exams.

Thus, intellectual exchange loses none of its intensity in distance learning, although teachers may sometimes feel frustrated by their lack of physical presence[31]. Paradoxically, this absence creates space for students to become autonomous. It is a Paschal experience: a pedagogical death and resurrection where the teacher withdraws to enable the learner to flourish.

Does distance teaching not essentially demonstrate a prerequisite for the learner's autonomy, namely the teacher's effacement or the transformation of their role[32]?

Our mission is not just to pass on knowledge, but also to nurture autonomous and creative thinkers who are connected to a thousand-year-old tradition.

The flipped classroom is a pedagogical model that reverses the traditional order of teaching. In a traditional course, the teacher imparts knowledge in the classroom (usually in the form of a lecture), and then the students complete exercises or practical work at home to consolidate this knowledge. In the flipped classroom, this dynamic is reversed.

Initially, students access course content (readings, videos, podcasts, etc.) at home at their own pace, before the class. These resources may include pre-recorded videos, readings, and other

---

[31] This experience inspired me to write "La théologie de la distance" (The Theology of Distance, see Appendix 3).

[32] John 16:7: *It is expedient for you that I go away [...]*.

teaching aids. They are encouraged to assimilate the theory and explore the concepts for themselves.

Secondly, group work begins for practical and interactive activities: class time is no longer devoted to theoretical explanation, but to the application of concepts. Students work together on projects, case studies and discussions. The teacher plays the role of facilitator, answering questions, helping to clarify difficult points and guiding practical activities.

Flipped learning emphasises students' autonomy and responsibility, allowing them to take ownership of the content before the lesson and to use class time to deepen their understanding through debate. This model encourages a more interactive relationship between teachers and students.

If our teaching method emphasises the written word, it is not to disregard the importance of oral expression, but to honour the spoken word: the spark can only fly when two flints of sufficient size can clash. Michel Henry had this intuition: in philosophy, we only really discuss things in writing. And if Socrates' words had the effect of a torpedo, of an electric shock, as certain fish produce, if the pedagogy of the Desert Fathers consisted in throwing out an enigmatic phrase for the disciple to ponder, turning it over in his mind as one turns an olive stone in his mouth, then this was not teaching. It was a Socratic method, a provocation to reminiscence or intuition, something akin to preaching, a call to intellectual and existential risk-taking, a provocation to produce a thought. This was the place of the mentor, the master, the rabbi, the starets, insofar as they had clearly understood that the aim was not to merely produce clones of themselves, but to awaken free, independent minds. His role was to encourage deep, personal reflection, rather than simply passing on ready-made knowledge to be repeated.

This kind of living word calls on us to go beyond certain thresholds, to cross boundaries, to take risks. It is like adults calling out to fledglings, afraid to leave their nest. In the flipped teaching method, the written word feeds the intelligence, gives wings, strengthens the muscles and makes the feathers grow. It transmits culture and instils the energy needed to soar, think, question and debate.

Digital writing allows constant updating, it does not freeze thought, but it extends and deepens the debate, offering a technical dimension and precision that oral communication does not achieve. Some seek to "found a school"; i.e., to reproduce themselves through their disciples. Yet Aristotle did not repeat Plato. The true loyalty of a disciple to their master does not consist in reproducing them identically. Irenaeus did not repeat Polycarp, who himself did not simply reproduce Saint John. Augustine did not copy Ambrose of Milan, any more than Thomas Aquinas repeated Albert the Great, or Congar his teacher Marie-Dominique Chenu.

How can we ensure that the transmission of knowledge takes place through lively debate that constantly bears new fruit? Interactivity is a concrete feature of each course, thanks to a forum where students can ask the teacher fundamental questions and receive answers not only from the teacher but also from other students. They also have access to previously published questions and answers. This process creates a collective memory of the exchanges, which sediments into fertile soil for future debates. At the end of the course, students can also propose contributions to enrich and complete the content, by adding personal work or referring to relevant works: a real "augmented course". For example, as part of the course on androgyny, which compares Plato's myth with the Genesis account of the creation of woman, a student shared a hypertext link to a comic strip available online, presenting the Greek myth in a playful and faithful way.

Another form of interactivity can be seen in the seminars. Around fifteen students undertake a research project under the guidance of a professor, in three stages of two weeks each. During the first week of each stage, the students make the proposed content their own and write a contribution. The second week is devoted to a debate on the forum around a question posed by the teacher. This formula combines the flexibility of asynchronous learning with interactivity, since the exchanges take place in real time, allowing responses to follow one another without delay.

A third form of interactivity is achieved when students meet directly with their mentors, or when students meet face-to-face with lecturers and members of the administration during our *Journées d'Études Participatives* (JEP, Participatory Study Days), colloquia or sessions. For PhD students, this interactivity is also expressed through the doctoral school's videoconferences, where methodological issues are discussed, as well as exchanges on cross-disciplinary themes. By recording these sessions, students can access these teaching resources in the form of podcasts, continually enriching the content over the years.

This interactivity strengthens the sense of belonging and encourages the formation of a genuine study and research community. After their studies, former students can maintain these links through the student community, an alumni network that enables them to continue to interact, by signing up for continuing education courses and taking part in face-to-face events such as the *Journées d'Études Participatives* (JEP, Participatory Study Days) or sessions. The newsletter plays an essential role in disseminating information. It should be noted that the associations, the Academic Senate, the teaching staff and the research groups have a good number of alumni among their members. This network could be further strengthened by improving communication about new courses, seminars, recent publications and face-to-face activities.

Teaching methods vary from culture to culture. In the Latin world, lecturing is the preferred method: the teachers present the summary that they have patiently worked out, and expect the student to memorise and reproduce the summary accurately.

In contrast, in the Anglo-Saxon world, and particularly in the Oxbridge model[33], the teacher does not write the course, but rather publishes it: publish or perish. It provides students with a portfolio of readings, offering various points of view that the student must synthesise or put into perspective in a personal way, by writing an essay. Here, less emphasis is placed on memory and more on critical and dialectical thinking and creative presentation.

In the much more verbal Latin American world, writing is often relegated to second place. Teachers prefer to use PowerPoint, with diagrams and images, and record themselves in an oral style that is often hesitant and redundant, addressing the audience as if they were

---

[33] The Oxford-Cambridge pairing.

present. The transmission is slower and less structured, but there is a greater sense of a living, almost intimate, communication.

Consulting learners about their preferences can prove useful. Watching a videoconference where the teacher reads out the text in a monotone voice is unbearable. Why not read it yourself, at your own pace, without having to take notes?

On the other hand, watching the teacher speak while benefiting from diagrams in the background can provide real added value. Short films on philosophy, theology, history, art history, law or medicine can also enrich the learning experience by making the concepts more concrete, almost like practical work. However, the written text remains central to the transmission of knowledge.

Kindness does not preclude clarity, the courage of intelligence, which enables us to face up to realities that we would sometimes prefer to ignore. Why do some teachers reject distance learning?

For some, it is simply that they do not feel capable of it. Although they can teach locally, they fear that they will not perform well on an international stage. This "natural selection" is not a problem in itself, but rather a solution.

The mistake would be to believe that it is merely a technical leap[34] involving the transposition of presentations into videos. Preparing notes for a classroom audience is relatively straightforward, whereas writing a lecture is an entirely different task. It must be finished to a standard comparable to a published book and offer a certain degree of novelty. Once published, it escapes its creator, just as a dove flies away when its cage is opened.

The preparation time, teaching method and final "product" are all different. It is a wholly different vocation.

Our institution does more than simply pass on *knowledge, skills and experience*; it *develops intellectual instruments and paradigms for action and thought that are useful for proclamation in a world marked by ethical and religious pluralism*[35].

---

[34] With Skype, Zoom, Teams or other software, the process is different.

[35] *Veritatis Gaudium*, see next page.

Moreover, it conceives and implements an innovative mode of transmission, adapted to a constantly changing technical and media world, that of the new generations. It exploits the formidable potential of AI, without denigrating it from the outset, as we did with the Internet in its early days. This new and constantly evolving tool for learning, researching and sharing knowledge is at the service of everyone, individuals and institutions alike.

Veritatis Gaudium

Pope Francis calls for a *radical paradigm shift and even a courageous cultural revolution:*

- Overcoming different divorces: between theology and pastoral care, faith and life;
- Going beyond the confines of our own diocese, to be ready in our hearts to preach the Gospel to the ends of the earth;
- An authentic culture of encounter, because truth is logos, which creates a dia-logos and therefore communication and communion;
- Transdisciplinarity, networking between different institutions;
- Open thinking, because the theologian who is satisfied with their complete and finished thought is a mediocre person.
- A radical paradigm shift and even a courageous cultural revolution.

To achieve this, Pope Francis wants the Church to develop a *mysticism of the people, a spirituality of global solidarity that springs from the mystery of the Trinity*. It is not just *a matter of passing on knowledge, skills and experience*, but *of developing intellectual instruments, paradigms for action and thought that are useful for proclamation in a world marked by ethical and religious pluralism*.

The mode of governance is decisive in maintaining a coherent direction over the long term. Our institution has chosen a model inspired by that of the Order of Preachers, and from the very first election it has been possible to check that the procedures are working well.

The Rector's term of office is five years, and their first responsibility is to preserve the unity of the institution, avoiding any fragmentation, whether this involves the isolation of languages taught or the compartmentalisation of faculties. The institution must be sufficiently centralised for internal exchanges to encourage cross-cultural and cross-disciplinary cross-fertilisation, but also sufficiently decentralised to ensure that innovations are not stifled by overly rigid structures.

With teleworking and automatic translation, the recruitment pool has opened up internationally, and consequently to the whole Order of Preachers. It is therefore possible to find competent and willing people to take on management responsibilities, whether in the Rectorate, deanery or general administration. Our institution's activities are directly in line with the Order's intellectual mission and fully in line with its priorities.

Teleworking is revolutionising not only teaching, but also its organisation. Our international team is particularly diverse. In 2021, it will include a British employee, Carly Wood, in Oslo, a Lebanese, Marie José Sarkis in Brussels, Br Augustin Williwoli, Dean of the Faculty of Philosophy in Kisangani in the DRC, Emmanuel Boissieu, Vice-Dean in Lyon and another Vice-Dean, Br Jorel François, Haitian, in Montpellier. The Dean of the Faculty of Social Sciences, Br Manuel Rivero, a Spaniard, was on Reunion Island, often on mission in Madagascar, while the Dean of Theology, Sr Evelyne Maurice, was in Bulle, Switzerland. An assistant to the rector and interpreter/translator, Rawad Al Feghali, lived in Beirut, the administrative director, Cécile Boucherle, lived in Aude, and the general secretary, Clémentine Franchi, lived in Douai. Caterina Erando, in charge of publishing, was based in Rome, while an English-speaking tutor was in the United States and another in England. The vice-rector, Br Ameer Jajé, was in Baghdad, the vice-rector, Sr Marie Monnet, in Brussels, and the rector in Corrèze. The trainees were based in Ivory Coast, Burkina Faso, Madagascar, Congo and Benin. Finally, the Communications Director, Ina Kasnija, based in Brussels, was of Albanian origin and Greek nationality. Naturally, she suggested Athens as a venue for a face-to-face meeting!

The face-to-face meetings always take place in symbolic locations, such as Israel and Jordan, in collaboration with the École Biblique et Archéologique Française de Jérusalem. Other sessions are planned in Lebanon, Turkey, Greece and Spain, countries where the three monotheistic religions have lived side by side for several centuries. These meetings create lasting links which, as experience has shown, help to weave the associative network of our institution.

Domuni is rooted in the Preachers' vocation to proclaim the Gospel. It is a desire, a passion, a vocation of transmission, based on study and listening. *Veritas* is the watchword of the Order of Preachers... A truth to which we must bear witness, not only by word (*verbo*), but also by example (*exemplo*). This means that we have to live this truth as much as we have to proclaim it, in keeping with the message. Because, as we keep saying, *the message is the medium*. From the outset, it was essential that the Gospel be proclaimed on the Net, that it enter this "digital continent" and be present in this new culture. This fact was a testimony in itself. The Internet was a challenge for preachers, and even if this aspect of novelty has disappeared today, the question remains: how can we be present on this terrain? Passing on the faith is always accompanied by a form of Passover and dispossession.

Our institution is a special kind of university. Most of the teaching staff are also active in face-to-face teaching in other training centres and share their local experience on our platform, remotely and internationally. The students, for their part, are often already professionals: doctors, engineers, lawyers, teachers, pastoral priests, etc. They are mature individuals who approach theology or philosophy with a wealth of experience. Three quarters of them are aged between 25 and 44.

The debate extends across teachers, students, disciplines, religions and cultures, and is further enriched by collaboration with partner universities.

This context creates a fundamental experience in theology as in philosophy: the encounter with the Other, with a lower or upper case "O"[36]. This is in line with Pope Francis' intention to encourage

---

[36] The thought of Emmanuel Levinas, the philosopher of relationships, has helped us a great deal in conceptualising our experience. Levinas challenges the claim to "know" that is the hallmark of Western science. He insists on the mystery of the person. A subject is always unknown; it is not an object. Levinas contrasts totality and infinity: a certain totalitarianism versus freedom. In Domuni's experience there is an element of vertigo, an opening onto the infinite, in the encounter with the other, with others who are irreducible to knowledge.

a *mysticism of the people*, a *spirituality of global solidarity that springs from the mystery of the Trinity.*

After this panoramic vision, this snapshot of the situation in 2023, let us now revisit our adventure by looking at its beginnings.

The genesis of the institution (1997-2005)

Protohistory

The spring, whispering around the pebbles, tells of the subterranean paths that the water has patiently travelled before smiling into the light. For the spring is never the first of its kind: something mysteriously precedes it. Thousands of small, invisible, silent trickles come together to form it. They do not form an isolated whole, but converge where the light begins.

What are these trickles that precede our stream? Like prehistory, the origins of our association emerge from a context, a convergence of factors. Each is essential, but none is sufficient on its own. In the same way that history only begins with the appearance of writing, it is from the moment Domuni was named that its path could be retraced. However, there is a prehistory to our project.

For men do not gather figs from off thorns[37]. The association was not conceived at random, nor by just anyone; it is imbued with a collective culture. It breathes a spirit: a compelling desire to share a common treasure, both intangible and spiritual, a passion for passing on a living heritage that regularly catches fire when it comes into contact with contemporary issues.

Our school certainly needed a range of skills – academic, IT and administrative – to take shape in a natural surge of generosity. But it also needed a context, a favourable atmosphere, and at that particular time of the beginnings of the Internet, a new wind was blowing: one that combined a taste for innovation with the choice of freedom, in a youthful openness to the joy of creation.

As the word suggests, a university embraces the universal, with interculturality and interdisciplinarity at the heart of its mission. An

---

[37] Word of Jesus. Lk 6:44.

authentic university offers full freedom to think, express oneself and teach. It experiences truth as an ongoing search, similar to that of children who move, without ever tiring of it, from one "Why?" to another "Why?", right up to "Why why?"

To be truly free, a university must be based on a democratic system, nourished by a democratic culture. To be open to all, it must offer scholarships to the less privileged. There is no question of reproducing a plutocracy by confiscating knowledge.

A self-respecting university does not isolate itself in the Platonic sky of abstract ideas; it confronts the issues of humanity, social problems (racism, gender, migration), political crises (war, peace, democracy), economic crises (poverty, trade imbalances). Its teaching is imbued with a reflection rooted in experience, as close to reality as possible.

Eight centuries of heritage

Domuni is driven by the same vision, the same mission, the same vocation as the Order of Preachers. They have the same genes, the same software. For eight centuries, it has created or helped to found numerous universities in Europe, Asia, the New World and now in Africa. Its networking gives it exceptional international experience. Its democratic experience has withstood the crises of history.

It would be interesting to reread *Le Feu sacré* (The Sacred Fire), in which Régis Debray cites the influence of the Dominicans on the evolution of institutions, in particular the American Constitution[38], and to reflect in this light on the "offbeat" side of utopians who put everything in common and offer a glimpse of the possibility of a different world: "another world" or "a world that has become other"? A utopia, a prophetic tension, a communism... Under what conditions?

Even if the history of the Order of Preachers includes some dark pages, it bears witness to a studious fraternity and a democratically structured international network. The Master of the Order is the only major superior in the Catholic Church whose election does not have to be confirmed by the Pope. From the first, local level, authority comes from below. The moderator

---

[38] "Seeking in the constitutions of preachers the means to better hear the American Constitution" Le Feu sacré (The Sacred Fire), Régis Debray, Gallimard, 2005, p. 75.

is appointed by the group for a limited time, assisted by a board that balances their powers in a kind of parliament. This democracy cultivates freedom of expression. As a mendicant order, the O.P. is naturally inclined to generosity. Its whole purpose is to proclaim the faith, preach the Gospel, enlighten the mind and seek the Truth.

The rest flows from this, taking shape in the fight for the oppressed, following the example of Brother Bartolomé de Las Casas, the founder of human rights; in the promotion of international law, following the example of Brother Francisco de Vitoria, whose bust and name are displayed in the Hall of Nations at the UN; following the example of Brother Joseph Delos, involved in the inception of the European Union. Dominicans have already explored many major themes: the meeting of religions (Br Serge de Beaurecueil in Kabul, the convent in Mosul, the IDEO in Cairo), social issues (Br Joseph Lebret, "Économie et Humanisme", Br Dominique Pire, Nobel Peace Prize winner in 1958, Br Henri Burin des Rosiers, lawyer in Brazil for landless peasants, etc.), the arts (Fra Angelico, Brother Marie-Alain Couturier), not to mention the Bible (Brother Joseph Lagrange, founder of the École Biblique de Jérusalem, archaeologist of Qumran), and theology (Albertus Magnus, Thomas Aquinas, Brothers Dominique Chenu, Yves Congar, E. Schillebeeckx, etc.).

As far as the Arab world is concerned, the Dominican history is rich. Of course, there is the convent in Cairo and the one in Jerusalem, but there is also a presence in Iraq that goes back to before the end of the Crusades.

The scope of the Order, in terms of both its purpose and its historical achievements, is too broad for any individual or community to honour all its nuances in a given place and time. Even a large province cannot carry the entire Order's project alone. Yet it feels its connaturality. The same is true of our university, which is therefore under the direct supervision of the Master of the Order.

In the beginning was the Word[39]. Saint Dominic once spent the night conversing with his innkeeper, who was a Cathar from Toulouse. Meeting others was at the heart of the apostle's life, regardless of their culture, beliefs or way of thinking. The process of dialogue is more important than its outcome. It is a way of life in itself that speaks volumes. As Brother Marcel Dubois, who took Israeli nationality after the 1948 war and taught philosophy at the Hebrew University of Jerusalem, pointed out, we have to start by

---

[39] Gospel of John, chapter 1, verse 1.

clearly identifying our points of contention: *what we agree to disagree on*. The aim is not to convince each other, but to talk to each other. When a family planning officer who has witnessed unwanted pregnancies, a monk and African priests with sometimes "macho" attitudes, and others meet to discuss issues affecting half the world's population, the points of view diverge profoundly. However, under the guidance of a wise teacher, these exchanges transform into a shared exploration based on mutual respect.

The Internet makes these intense encounters possible. For instance, a young Christian family man living in Mali who is threatened with death by jihadists can find a natural affinity with a Pakistani or an Iraqi when talking about interfaith dialogue. This dialogue, nourished by profoundly different experiences, can offer Europeans, who are dealing with tensions of their own, new perspectives.

Do not be fooled into thinking that distance hinders communication; experience shows that boundaries reassure and foster trust. *It is the forbidden that enables expression.* At a seminar on comparative religions organised by the Lumen Vitae International Centre, during which I discussed magic from a Voodoo perspective, the participants began to speak[40] openly. We discovered that a superior had used magic to get elected, how this had been uncovered and punished, and that politicians had also used magic for the same purpose. Such transparency would never have been achieved if the people we spoke to had been sitting in the same room together.

As Pierre Claverie[41] used to say, the Order's project is to be *present on the fault lines*. At the heart of the O.P. is a passion for engaging with others. This mission is rooted in the heart of the Trinity: one God in three persons. *As the Father hath loved Me, so have I loved you. Continue ye in My love.* The ministry of the Word is not just another service: we lend our bodies to it and are inextricably linked to it. The medium is not a mere instrument. It colours the message to the point that it becomes the message itself. If the way in which we deliver something is more important than the

---

[40] To write*, I am sorry, but this slip of the tongue bears such significance!

[41] Dominican, Bishop of Oran, assassinated on 1 August 1996.

thing itself, the way in which we speak can be revealing, as can the way in which we remain silent in certain situations. Poverty, vulnerability and dependence are inherent to the Gospel when it is passed on. To depart from it is to betray it. Domuni is a theological project in itself; it is also a "theological place". It bears witness to a certain "spirit". To write its history is to give an account of a vocation: "The call is only heard in the response itself"[42].

To begin with, we had modestly envisaged creating a network bringing together the Dominican study centres with the Catholic institutes at its heart. Convinced that it would require a great deal of human resources – teachers and computer specialists – and therefore financial resources far beyond our capacities, we thought that no institute could achieve this alone. It was in this spirit that we brought together the deans of the French theology faculties to present our idea. But to our great surprise, they were far from grasping the potential of the new technologies, treating our proposal as if it were simply a question of creating yet another little distraction. Faced with this lack of vision, we mobilised our own resources to gradually build up a website and put together a series of courses.

Without taking ourselves too seriously, we presented these lessons not as "courses", but as "hiking trails", because theology, for our contemporaries, should be a pleasure, even a luxury. It had to be "fun", as the Americans say: playful and open to all. Structured by professionals like Brother H. Ponsot and our first IT specialist, our institution has grown thanks to the commitment of passionate volunteers.

We started out as a group of institutions and we had to go it alone. We brought together volunteer teachers on an autonomous teaching platform, ready to develop its own network around it. In fact, we were not starting from scratch. *The function creates the body*. It was the need for resources that revealed the wealth of teaching material in our libraries, drawers and hard drives, and we had to make the most of it. New teachers were coming forward.

---

[42] *Levinas, Autrement qu'être ou au-delà de l'essence* (Otherwise Than Being or Beyond Essence), The Hague: M. Nijhoff, 1974, p. 190 – quoted in J.-L. Chrétien, L'Appel et la réponse, p. 41.

If faith is not communicated, it dies, because it is in the nature of faith to spread. The Second Vatican Council says that *the nature of the Church is to be missionary*, which means that a Church that is not missionary is distorted. In the absence of resources, we have followed Thomas Aquinas' maxim: *All thou canst, do thou endeavour*[43]. We dared, we took risks and we persevered. One of Jesus' statements surprised me. He told his disciples that they would do greater works than he had done[44]. How was that possible? *Herein is My Father glorified, that ye bear much fruit [...]*[45]. The Internet allowed us to multiply our efforts and, since *the harvest was bountiful and the labourers few*, we introduced the combine harvester!

Universities were born out of theology faculties

In France, we often forget that it was these faculties that gave rise to the first universities. During a trip to New York to present Domuni's application to become an ECOSOC organisation of the United Nations, we took the opportunity to visit several American universities in the region[46]. In each instance, we delved into their annals, with a particular focus on their genesis, and it came as something of a revelation to discover that many of them had their inception in the living room of a pastor, imparting theological instruction to a select few[47].

Our journey has not been a "long, quiet river". Let us go back to the source and use the metaphor of a torrent. When it comes to

---

[43] *Quantum potes, tantum aude* (in the hymn *Lauda Sion*, verse 2).

[44] Jn 14:12: *Verily, verily I say unto you, he that believeth in Me, the works that I do he shall do also; and greater works than these shall he do, because I go unto My Father. And whatsoever ye shall ask in My name, that will I do, that the Father may be glorified in the Son. If ye shall ask anything in My name, I will do it. If ye love Me, keep My commandments.* Jesus insists: this is not optional.

[45] Jn 15:8.

[46] No, I did not just "come out of Harvard", as many people have done; I also "came out of Yale", Columbia, Princeton and MIT because I went to visit them!

[47] Harvard: *In its early days, the school had just nine students and one professor, Nathaniel Eaton... Harvard trained many pastors.* (Wikipedia, Harvard), Yale: *A group of ten Congregationalist ministers [...] who were all Harvard alumni, met at the study of the Reverend Samuel Russell in Branford, Connecticut, to pool their books in order to form the school's first library.* (Wikipedia, Yale)

speed, the opposite is true: a mountain stream flows much faster than a river on the plains. For our project, however, it is the other way around. The pace quickens over time, whereas at the start everything is slow and winding. It takes 50 metres of snow for a glacier to start moving out of its accumulation basin. It takes many courses and teachers to structure an academic curriculum. The mystery of the source lies in the fact that students and teachers appear simultaneously from the outset, as if recognition occurred even before the institution was established. Without this recognition, there would be no interest in enrolling, and without enrolments, the institution could not exist. The chicken and the egg must emerge at the same time.

This mysterious zone is the accumulation basin, where the miracle occurs when snow falls abundantly from elsewhere above. It is a cold, dark and secret universe. The only thing left to do is cross the "glacial lock", which has its first critical point at the bergschrund: the initial crevasse that forms when the ice begins to advance, separating it from the stable accumulation area. It took five years to achieve this first objective: the creation of a master's degree in theology.

Luckily, we were in an ecological niche with very little competition. For French people studying theology, quality took precedence over the diploma. Lay people did not study the subject to make a profession out of it, and teachers practised it as a vocation.

In 2000, during a visit to the convent for an anniversary, Father André Dupleix, then rector of the Catholic University of Toulouse, agreed to come up to my office for a few minutes to look at the website on my screen. He looked at it with an amused expression. Through the reflection of his glasses, I felt as if I had been transported back to my childhood, when I would throw a stick into a stream, following it as if it were a majestic ocean liner.

In fact, I could already see Domuni as it is today, in the estuary we know. Strong intuitions carried me through time. They projected me decades ahead into a transformed reality: a world where the ice had melted, the tributaries had joined the current and water flowed under the bridges until a mighty river covered the memory of that modest torrent, which carefree children had tried to dam with a few pebbles.

After the estuary, the metaphor evolved into that of the ocean. With the internet, we were on a new continent and the question was one of inculturation: adapting to the culture specific to this new medium. Having experienced Latin American culture, more specifically in Cusco, the capital of the *Tawantin Suyu*[48] and the heart of Quechua culture, I was familiar with the effort to inculturate.

This mountainous region, where the roads never ceased to wind, had a very different relationship with space and time to that experienced in Europe, where a linear perception of movement is predominant.

The Andean civilisation questioned the centre of space, and I saw a possible link with the idea of recapitulation in the Epistle to the Ephesians[49]. This cosmovision stimulated me because it approached space and time differently to Western thought. In the West, the future lies ahead and the past behind. For the Quechua, however, the future lies behind because it cannot be seen, while the past lies ahead because it can be observed. This cultural sensitivity prompted me to reflect more deeply on the distant and asynchronous dimensions that characterise our teaching.

I had followed the debates in the 70s and 80s about the inculturation of the Gospel. It was certainly no longer a question of translating the Gospel into Japanese, Chinese, Creole or Quechua. It was no longer a question of identifying the rites, symbols and values available as building blocks for a mixed-race theology, even though I loved preaching using the Inca imagination. It was a question of using an emerging technology, like writing, then printing, then radio, then television[50], to announce news that was always new, a surprise that was always surprising.

To establish its relevance, I would point out that, in the Gospel, Jesus sends his disciples out two by two, without a penny or food,

---

[48] The Inca Empire, made up of four *suyus*, regions, and a centre, *ombligo del mundo*, navel: Cusco.

[49] Eph 1:10: ...*that in the dispensation of the fullness of times He might gather together in one all things in Christ, both which are in heaven and which are on earth, even in Him.*

[50] In 1948, Father Raymond Pichard, a Dominican, founded "Le jour du Seigneur" (The Lord's Day), the televised Mass: https://www.lejourduseigneur.com. It is an interesting precedent.

with a staff, a single tunic and a single pair of sandals. He insists on the manner, on the conditions, and says nothing about the content. He says nothing about what is to be announced. Just as *the way you give matters more than what you give*, the way you communicate matters more than what you say: it is the way you communicate that constitutes the main content. *The message is the medium...*

Our message would therefore be to be present on the digital continent. And, like the poverty of the apostles, the simple fact of being accessible on the Net from the outset would speak volumes.

What were we going to call our "domain"? Nothing yet existed, either in concrete or legal terms; it was all a matter of intuition, intention and project. Giving it a name would make it possible to identify this initiative, even before organising it and giving it substance. I knew how important the choice of name was. I had observed the creation of COINCIDE, the federation of NGOs in the Cusco region, a neologism that perfectly expressed the essence of its mission. Following this example, we had to find an evocative word, a name that, like the Hebrew names, would reflect the profound being of what we were creating.

I suggested "UNIDO", a word that did not exist in French, formed from the first letters of UNIversité DOminicaine (Dominican University). Having recently landed in Toulouse, I was still thinking in Spanish. Unido is an unusual word, because it is generally used in the plural: "Somos unidos", because unity implies diversity. To be united, you need to be many. When it is used in the singular, it evokes a strengthened unity, an accomplished unity. And in my initial intuition, it already was, in a way. It was "virtually" so, because the whole project was digital, virtual, according to the terms used at the time, which varied depending on the language.

In the virtual world, we were not the first. An investigation revealed that the domain name UNIDO had already been taken, and not by just anyone: it had been reserved by the United Nations! That is when Hervé Ponsot suggested reversing the terms: DOMUNI. "Uni", as in University, indicated our initial project, and "DOM" illustrated the institution behind it. In English, it sounded perfect: "DOMinican UNIversity".

To the ear, the whimsical pronunciations of "Domuni" make up a veritable bouquet of expressions, each with its own charm. Sometimes you can hear "Domooni", with a soft "u". Others gravitate towards "Démuni" (destitute in French), which, despite its pejorative connotation, draws us closer to those to whom we extend grants. "Dimini" is quite meek, and so quite apt for a mendicant order. "Dominus" sounds a little pretentious, while "Dimono" evokes a judoka's kimono. In Italian, "Domani" (tomorrow) refers to the near future, and "Domino" to a black and white board game, alluding to the Dominicans' colours. This could however be a cause for concern: what if the domino effect topples everything in its path? We would have to imagine a reverse "domino effect", one that straightens things up instead of knocking them down. We even heard a meowing "Dominou", which would mean "DoKitten" in French. And why not? Dominou, the purring mascot, soft to the touch, dressed all in black and white, a genuine cat-monk! But who would have given it a mouse to go online with? Now that is a picture that needs painting: Dominou, a clever animal!

So, it was Br Hervé Ponsot who came up with the name "Domuni". Allow me to introduce him.

Brother Hervé Ponsot, O.P.

I am a brilliant all-rounder, he liked to say with disarming simplicity. And it is hard to argue with the facts. Frank, straightforward, he was everywhere at once, impossible to ignore. He seemed to know everything about everything and was quick to share his knowledge, as long as you were polite and did not interrupt him. He marvelled at his own abilities, and you shared with him the providential pleasure of having the chance to listen to him. He was undoubtedly right, because he was not content with words: he carried out complex tasks in the technical, human resources, accounting, administrative and even academic fields. He published scholarly articles.

His voice, deep and warm, sometimes seemed to hiccup. It was as if another voice, from elsewhere, was trying to butt in to approve, to applaud. This phenomenon remained mysterious and intriguing.

THE GENESIS OF THE INSTITUTION (1997-2005)

He sweated profusely, so he always had a light-coloured cloth towel on hand, that he constantly passed over his forehead, neck and hands. We felt sorry for him, we suffered for him, and we forgave him for not being able to achieve greater perfection. He was endearing, even if, always on the move, he constantly eluded you, just as he seemed to elude himself. It was impossible for him to walk normally; he always had to hurry, hunched over, as if driven by an inner urgency. The nickname "NHervé" (for "énervé", angry in French), an easy diminutive, did not do justice to the richness of his personality. Overbooked, rushed to the point of exhaustion, he regretted a superficiality that he felt was inevitable. He would so much have liked to delve deeper, to delve into everything. But despite this whirlwind, he never lacked humility – immense humility! He was a living spectacle.

He was not affected by the angst of failure that plagues so many of our communities. He would never go into all the reasons why our project might fail, nor would he discourage us before we had even started. On the contrary, thanks to his cheerful disposition, his feverish enthusiasm was infectious. It was this dynamism that, when I was elected provincial, led me to choose him as my *socius*, my right-hand man and my replacement during my stays abroad. When I shared with him the idea of creating an online theological training course for people who lived far from universities and could not travel to Europe or the United States, he welcomed the proposal enthusiastically, describing it as "brilliant" – I can still hear him today. Without wasting any time, he set to work: he created the website, developed an initial course on Saint Paul, and spread the idea, giving it substance.

Even though he mentioned in his final report that he had had to put the brakes on me on a number of occasions, I never sensed any resistance or inertia on his part. On the contrary, his commitment was complete.

When I phoned him in October 2023 to ask him for memories and anecdotes, he had forgotten a lot: *my memory is very poor*. He fondly remembered the early days: *it was Steve Job! Not in a garage, but almost!*

A self-taught computer scientist, Hervé created the first website and recruited the first intern, who went on to become an employee. He placed articles in a wide variety of media, like birth announcements announcing the project. A two-page photo in *Point de vue et images du monde* showed him enthroned in the cloister of the Jacobins in Toulouse, dressed in the grand Dominican habit, a laptop on his lap. The image caused quite a stir: it symbolised the alliance of tradition and modernity.

The numerous articles obtained by Hervé Ponsot

They are almost all there, newspapers from France and many from abroad: *Le Berry républicain, La Montagne, L'Est Éclair, La Dépêche, Le Monde, La Vie, La Croix, Libération, La Tribune, Les Echos, Le Midi libre, Le Pèlerin, Point de vue images du monde, VSD, Le Bulletin de l'archevêché de Montréal, Sainte Rita magazine, L'Amitié Dominicaine, Concorde, Point de Repère, Chrétiens en Morbihan, Le Télégramme, Ouest France, Notre Dame de la Trinité, le Web Magazine, L'Appel* (Belgium), *Dominicus, L'Avvenire, Famiglia Cristiana* (Italy), *Wort ant unWort* (Germany), *International Herald Tribune, The Chronicle of Higher Education* (USA), *List* (Polish), not forgetting the one written in Chinese ideograms.

The cartoons evoke the student and his computer, diplomas and the square caps of Anglo-Saxon academics! Few births have been celebrated with such media coverage. From the outset, all the elements were in place: the university, the international dimension, distance learning, e-learning and tutoring, all emphasising the term "Dominicans", which is often associated with "from Toulouse". Brother Hervé Ponsot appeared in the photos in religious garb, giving the project a face as a cyber-monk, cyber-theologian and cyber-evangelist.

In the articles, the word "university" is used in every language, even Chinese: *the Dominicans' online university, the Dominicans' university on the Internet, the virtual university of the Dominicans of Toulouse, the Dominicans develop the virtual university*[51]. As the weekly *La Vie* points out: *Domuni is a genuine online university, offering teaching...; www.domuni.eu is an online university offering teaching inherited from almost eight centuries of Dominican*

---

[51] *La Croix*, February 2005.

*tradition*⁵². In Italian, we speak of *Università domenicana via Internet, la prima università virtuale di teologia nel mondo*⁵³.

Dominicans are called *hip*⁵⁴. Brother Hervé Ponsot leads a team of *cyber-monks on the Internet*⁵⁵, and some articles go so far as to say that *the Internet is his religion*⁵⁶. He proposes *The Gospel of Fiber Optics*⁵⁷ and asks the question: *Is God an Internet user?* ⁵⁸ Journalists do not hesitate to headline: *Internet, promised land of the future?*⁵⁹ Or even *Net-theology, according to Dominic*⁶⁰.

In the midst of all this media hype, let us ask ourselves a fundamental question: why did we develop online distance learning? It all stemmed from an obvious observation: it was not right for future Latin American theologians to be forced to spend long periods of time in Europe for their training.

In a country as vast as Peru – whose surface area is equivalent to that of France, the UK and Spain combined – it was abnormal that it should be impossible to study theology up to Master's level, let alone doctorate level. The need for a Peruvian – and we had seen several examples of bitter failure – to return to their homeland after having been expatriated to Fribourg, Rome or Madrid for many years, often provoked a devastating internal earthquake.

---

[52] *La Vie*, April 2015

[53] *Avvenire*, October 10 1998

[54] *La Vie*, April 8, 1999.

[55] *La Dépêche*.

[56] *Of course, we already knew about soldier monks, builder monks, farmer monks and spirit-maker monks. Pilgrim monks and fake advertising monks who celebrate the virtues of a few cheeses on TV. But a monk surfing the Internet like a Silicon Valley pro? Now that is an entirely new one! And yet, this monk exists, I have met him, he is Brother Hervé, or Hervé Ponsot for short... From his cell, he perpetuates the tradition of the copyist monks of the Middle Ages, in High Tech version.* Article of unidentified origin, available in the archives.

[57] *Sainte Rita*, October 2003.

[58] *La Montagne*.

[59] *VSD*, December 2000.

[60] *La Vie*, March 16, 2006.

Those who remained religious after this forced acculturation no longer had the energy to experience this uprooting in reverse again, especially as their country had changed so much in their absence.

Furthermore, the financial cost of such a move was prohibitive, making it an option available to very few students. Was it inevitable that theology should be marked by this academic and, above all, cultural dependence? Was this not a remnant of persistent ecclesial colonialism[61]?

It was essential to enable preachers and theologians to train academically while remaining in their own countries. Thanks to the new medium, those who lived far from a university center could now study, while still being able to travel occasionally, without losing their social and cultural roots.

Once the obstacle of distance had been overcome, the question of financing remained. A business model had to be devised that was virtually free. *You received for free, give for free.* What is shared is not taken away from anyone. On the Internet, we pool more than we "share", in the sense that everyone takes their share exclusively. In a traditional library, readers have to follow one another; in a digital library, they can all read the same content simultaneously. The digital tool is "generous" and encourages volunteering. If a loaned book can be read fifty times, a book put online can be read an infinite number of times.

In keeping with this approach, an asceticism was called for: that of simplicity. Simplify procedures, favor short circuits, whether in communications or administration. No fear of automation, which would sooner or later lead to full telecommuting. No need for lecture halls, physical libraries or traditional offices. Does the face-to-face meeting still retain its charm for building trust and smoothing communication? If so, nomadism is reversed: it is no longer students who travel en masse, but a few teachers. Long live savings, long live ecology! Furthermore, partner institutions offer suitable locations for

---

[61] Cf. my course *L'Église d'Amérique latine est-elle encore européenne ?* (Is the Latin American Church Still European?)

direct contact, local tutoring, access to libraries, doctoral defenses and examinations.

Pope Francis often reminds us that time prevails over space[62]. By changing our relationship with space, we have in fact transformed our relationship with time. In seeking to reach those who live far from universities by offering training courses entirely at a distance, we have, without having anticipated it, reached another category of deprived people: the time-poor, those whose family and professional constraints limit their availability.

The change in the relationship to time, thanks to mainly asynchronous teaching, has had a major impact: financial autonomy. Why are some people time-poor? Because they are working! And what is the result? They are solvent! By exchanging their time for money, they acquire the means to pay their tuition fees. In a well-thought-out economic model, their contributions not only keep the institution running, but also provide scholarships for those who sorely lack the means to study.

With the idea of university, came quite naturally that of network. "University" refers to the adjective "universal", in keeping with the image of the international net, the "Web". In an article entitled "Le décollage de l'université virtuelle européenne" ("The Take-Off of the European Virtual University"), Les Échos states in its subtitle: *Without leaving their campus, students will be able to study courses at the universities of their choice*[63]. Libération sees a danger: *globalisation is pleased to announce its latest avatar: the global education market. Over 3,000 education and training professionals... have gathered in Vancouver (Canada) for the first World Education Market*[64].

Ensuring international coherence is at the heart of the mission of the Order's highest authorities. That is why, right from the start, when I was staying with my family in Ambleteuse, near Boulogne sur mer, I sent an e-mail straight to Rome.

---

[62] "Time is greater than space", *Amoris Laetitia*, no. 3.
[63] *Les Échos*, supplement, April 20, 1999.
[64] *Libération*, December 11 and 12, 1999.

Modems did not yet exist, and neither did smartphones. My computer was connected to a landline, the hesitant hum of which still echoes in my ear. Brother Timothy Radcliffe was quick to express his enthusiasm and encouragement. A year and a half later, on November 25 1999, the Master of the Order of Preachers sent an official letter to the provincials of Toulouse, Spain, Aragon, Canada and Chicago. It read almost like an order: "I am asking you...", a particularly strong formula.

> *I am asking you to set up a network... a simple, flexible structure... that would make it possible to exchange units of value. This structure should have minimal operating costs and aim to be self-financing. It should, of course, be such that other institutions could easily join in...*
>
> *I sincerely hope that you will take the next step and reach an agreement as soon as possible, so that this network of Dominican centers can actually be set up. In fact, other Catholic centers will very soon be present on the Internet, and it is important to be able to situate ourselves in relation to them as soon as possible, and to envisage a fruitful formation with them. When the question arises of official recognition of the titles issued by this new network of Dominican teaching centers, the Assistant for Intellectual Life will help you in your dealings with the Congregation for Catholic Education...*[65]

Above the Master of the Order is the General Chapter, which meets every three years to define the direction and priorities of the Order. The Bologna General Chapter, in July 1998, marked the beginning of an almost unbroken chain of support. Seven months before the official creation of the as yet unnamed association, the Chapter already congratulated the project's creators and encouraged its development: Domuni is above all a collective adventure, promoted by the general chapter.

> *79. The Chapter encourages the creation of an Internet university in the humanities, philosophy and theology. It thanks the Provinces that are helping to bring it about,*

---

[65] The letter is so well written that I can only guess that it was written by Brother Guido Vergauwen, then Assistant to the Master of the Order for Intellectual Life.

especially the Province of Toulouse, which provided the initial impetus and conception for the project.

Recommendation

80. The Chapter recommends that the brothers participate in the realisation of this project by teaching through this new medium, which will enable them to place themselves at the service of many students. The brothers are also called upon to make this project known, so that it can be enriched by numerous collaborators, both within and outside the Order, and widely offered to students who might be interested.

In response to the demand for the creation of a university network, the very first agreement was signed during the year with the Dominican College of Ottawa, following a "virtual" meeting, as it was then known. Thanks to the enthusiasm that brother Hervé Ponsot had managed to communicate to our neighbors, the Dominican convent in Rangueil was closely connected with Toulouse's very secular science university, Paul Sabatier. The prospect of sharing library files had enabled us to leapfrog the street and the ideological prejudices that separated us. Our project thus benefited from exceptional bandwidth[66] and the most professional technical support.

It was my very first Internet videoconference. On the screen appeared our partners from Ottawa, brothers Michel Gourgues and Maxime Allard from the *Dominican University College*. They had just got up, while for us, the working day was almost over. Despite a few interruptions, we could hear them clearly. The Quebec accent reminded us of the distance, even though we seemed to be in the same room. Their openness to new technologies was a source of great satisfaction to us. We shared the same vision, the same dream: simple, accessible and achievable.

The undersea cable was working perfectly, but there was still a cultural gap to be bridged. Our Canadian friends, who were French-speaking but came from an Anglo-Saxon cultural background, emphasised the importance of interactivity. Merely memorising lectures was not an option. Following the example of Oxford and Cambridge universities, teachers would suggest readings – articles or

---

[66] A term used at the time to describe the quality of a connection.

book chapters – that students would have to read and understand before producing their own summaries in the form of essays. This approach helped us teach other languages, which led to the idea of interactive seminars.

Gradually, technical tools became available to facilitate dialogue, such as forums, chats, Skype, Zoom and Teams. This first meeting marked a decisive step. We embraced the challenges of this new technical and intercultural landscape. The Internet was beginning to connect people, and our international network was gradually taking shape!

While our colleagues in the Americas were open to progress, minds in France were not yet ready to embrace new technologies or commit to inter-institutional collaboration. I have never forgotten the meeting of the deans of theology from the various Catholic institutes in France, where, paradoxically, I was not present. It was probably in 1999 in Paris at the convent on the Rue du Faubourg Saint-Honoré, where Brother Hervé Ponsot had invited them. Brother Luc-Thomas Somme was also there. The aim was ambitious: to create a common platform for online theology.

The Dominicans wanted to share their ideas and implement them alongside existing teaching institutions. The idea of developing the project independently had not even crossed their minds. However, together, everything seemed within reach; all they had to do was pool their existing intellectual resources and make them accessible online. With the enthusiasm typical of the Mendicant Orders and the vigour of the early days, Brother Hervé was aiming for complete free access. We were imbued with the optimism of startups, the notion of universal globalisation.

But questions from the theology deans quickly dispelled the brothers' euphoria. *What would it cost per student?* asked one of the deans. *Which region of France would be affected?* continued another. Their inability to even imagine the project made the meeting almost absurd. Brother Hervé replied wryly: *We did not offer you to buy tickets, but to help us build the locomotive.* As for the region concerned, the very nature of the project, being in the *cyberspace*, made the question irrelevant.

I remember the minutes of that meeting: you never forget such a disappointment. Stubbornly, I managed to get a meeting with the director of the Centre Sèvres[67]. Surely the Jesuits would understand! At the end of my talk, the young director proudly announced that they had come up with the same idea: they were going to give each of their teachers an email address (!). I could not speak any further; my proposal was simply inaudible. I cannot forget this failure: our project could very well have ended there.

Since there was no way of sharing our enthusiasm for this common horizon, we had to go it alone. We initially believed that we needed other institutions because we lacked sufficient resources, but we discovered that this was not the case. In fact, our resources were already there; we just had to take an inventory of them and make them available. What were these resources?

First and foremost, intelligence and generosity, two virtues that complement and reinforce each other. Then there were the articles, lectures and past courses, whether handwritten, typescript or digitised. Many teachers had responded to our appeal on a voluntary basis. It was then that a distinction collapsed in my mind: the opposition between progressives and conservatives. The latter, against all odds, had willingly embraced the modernity of the "digital continent", contributing unreservedly.

We found on several occasions that, for an institution rooted in face-to-face teaching, the transition to distance learning was as difficult as for a car to start flying. In general, one third of teachers were prepared to try the experiment, while the other two thirds refused, fearing an increase in workload or a reduction in salary. Individual meetings with teachers became a priority, pushing collaboration with institutions down the list of priorities.

We have observed this phenomenon with the Institut Catholique d'Angers, the Irish at the Priory Institute, the Angelicum in Rome, and practically all the faculties with which we have been in contact. The decision to teach entirely at a distance made our school a veritable alien.

---

[67] The Jesuit Faculty of Theology, now the "Faculté Loyola Paris".

In other words, distance learning was perceived as an entirely different beast from face-to-face teaching. We embodied what was called a *disruptive innovation*, comparable to the introduction of digital technology in photography as opposed to film. In this regard, it was informative to examine the history of Kodak, which, despite having developed the digital camera, could not modify its manufacturing design to withstand this transformation.

A successful start-up

80% of start-ups that started with a bang in the last decade of the twentieth century have fizzled out. They were founded on an opportunity, usually technological, a risk and an investment, but because of the lack of profitability, investors quickly withdrew. Companies valued in the billions went bankrupt in a matter of months.

Domuni is a start-up that survived, perhaps because it was not dependent on any investors and grew very slowly.

Suddenly, faced with a lack of support and the weariness of the first employee, Hervé distanced himself from the company in November 2001. At the time, he was seriously ill[68], and I did not realise how important his withdrawal was. It was only in 2024, while sorting through the archives for this book, that I discovered his long letter dated 13 November 2001[69]. After two years of intense activity,

---

[68] I underwent surgery in the USA during the Providence General Chapter in July 2001, but I suffered an N.D.E. following a nosocomial infection which became apparent nine months later and required a new operation.

[69] See the long letter that Hervé Ponsot sent to the members of the Board of Directors on 13 November 2001. He proposed a different project, Domuni "2nd draft", consisting of seminars. He explained that A. had lost interest and was retiring. In the 2nd version of the project, A. would no longer be our employee, but a service provider, paid by the seminar participants. He concluded his letter by saying *It seems to me that we have a choice between two policies: 1. Let the university project stand on its own merits and enrich it gradually with various contributions, particularly from Catholics. However, I remain sceptical about Catholics' ability to "do something", even among the most motivated. Then, when the time comes, start again from scratch with a stronger pedagogical approach and greater participation from students and teachers. It will come as no surprise to you to learn that this is my clear preference. 2. If you want to achieve more,*

Hervé was throwing in the towel. It was at this critical moment that I took over, because in my vision of apostolic preaching, a lack of resources was an inevitable part of the preacher's role.

Appointed Director of the École Biblique et Archéologique de Jérusalem (EBAF), Hervé radically severed ties with Domuni, which would never have seen the light of day without his brilliant introduction *in fanfare*[70].

Having introduced the man without whom none of this would have been possible, the author of this book must now reveal the personal elements that enabled him to go on and write the following pages of this story.

Brother Michel Van Aerde

At the age of five, I had a singular experience: that of a natural and delicate harmony, which I gradually identified as a discreet presence, whom I came to address as "you". I cultivated this special relationship, while constantly asking myself: why me? And above all: why not others too?

It is not comfortable to be inhabited by a passion for life that is born precisely when, for most people, it ceases to be perceptible. When I was a teenager, I considered becoming a Trappist monk. My sceptical, anti-clerical father's fierce opposition made me wait until I reached the age of majority, then set at twenty-one. To prove that my vocation was no illness, folly or mere escapism, I enrolled in a preparatory course for the Grandes Écoles at Sainte-Geneviève in Versailles. There, I lived through May 1968 to the fullest, before leaving for India for the summer.

Already passionate about yoga and the great gurus, I undertook this trip for a completely different reason. The Jesuits were

---

which is possible, you must guarantee it by securing funding, ensuring you can find teachers and guaranteeing a real commitment from Catholics. You must also find help or a successor for A. These are heavy tasks! Which I, for one, will not accept under any circumstances!

[70] Expression of Brother Augustin Laffay, O.P.

organising a micro-cooperation between Indian and French students. For two summer months, we camped in the middle of a desert near Madras (now Chennai), to build a dispensary in a village of untouchables (*dalits*).

We also took it in turns to set off in small groups to discover this immense country, each state having its own particularities. I would need several books to tell the story of May 1968, the discovery of India, yoga and Hinduism, as well as my experiences in Calcutta, in the care homes, *City of Joy*[71], and the confrontation with misery.

In October 1969, I entered the École Nationale Supérieure d'Agronomie de Montpellier (ENSAM, Montpellier National School of Agronomy). During the holidays, I spent extended periods at the Trappist Abbey of Aiguebelle. With two friends, I also embarked on a tour of Cistercian monasteries across France.

Studying very specific sciences for five years took its toll on me. Geology taught me to think in terms of millions of years, genetics taught me about the evolution of living organisms, and rural economics taught me about the conditions of development in an international context. Climate plays an important role. You also need to understand predators, whether insects, fungi or wild animals, and analyse marketing channels and soil erosion problems. Throughout, you must pay particular attention to the limiting factors, such as working time, farm size, water, tools, seeds, their cost and quality, and, of course, the market. This training provided me with a broad perspective and the ability to synthesise information efficiently. I then specialised and became a "generalist".

Later, as I had to study philosophy and then theology (i.e., the history of thought) I also became a scientist-literary. I do not want to hear about any identity problems!

There are many reasons for that. Some people call me "Padre" or "Father", even though I have no children. I was born in Douai, in the north of France, but I studied in Montpellier and then Toulouse. I was the first boy born French in my family. My father, Stanley, was born in the United States. As for my surname, it belongs to a language

---

[71] Dominique Lapierre, *City of Joy*, Robert Laffont, Paris, 1985.

I do not know, I only know that it means "of the earth", which does not indicate a specific place.

Nothing in there suggested I would one day be the founder of a university. I passed each year with such low grades that I was given compulsory holiday homework. Throughout my secondary education, I never achieved an average grade in French.

Because of my nervousness, the large number of pupils per class (sometimes 45) and the lack of air, I was literally suffocating. I would leave for school before dawn and would not return until after sunset, so I still remember those school years as long, dark tunnels. On the other hand, sunny holidays opened my mind and taught me about real life.

In preparatory classes, I often escaped by pressing a thumb to one ear while the other was plugged with a ball of wax. From time to time, I would take my hand away to listen to where the lesson was going, but mostly I read a book on my lap, living my studies as a secondary activity.

When I joined the Dominicans, I asked to become a cooperator brother, wishing to be at the service of these intellectual brothers who impressed me with their ability to express themselves in public. My inferiority complex was dispelled when I obtained a bachelor's degree in philosophy in one year, followed by a master's the following year, while continuing my theology studies. From then on, I developed the conviction that, if I did not understand a document, it was because it was badly conceived or badly written, and not because I lacked ability.

Some students will forever remember certain teachers. In my case, it was the chaplain at the Faculty of Science and the Grandes Écoles in Montpellier, who was a true preacher. A doctor of law and theology, Brother Jacques Martin had served as an officer in the Algerian War, where he was awarded the Croix de Guerre, before joining the Order of Preachers. He was a personality of immense culture, who preached remarkably well.

In the small group of students he led, many discovered faith in the living, risen Christ. I marvelled at the sight of a God who came to meet people, a God who revealed himself. I experienced the Spirit at work in cities and in human culture, not just in a rural spiritual laboratory set in medieval aesthetics. I was becoming a contemplative in action, accompanying neophytes as they became aware of what was happening to them. They had received the whole package. All that remained was for them to unpack it, to take stock of what it contained, in a spiritual Socratic method in which I was involved.

After the novitiate and studies in philosophy at the University of Montpellier, followed by three years of theology in Toulouse, I returned to Montpellier where I set up as a student chaplain. At first, it was informal, as no one had hired me: I would put up posters myself to invite people to meetings to reflect on the Gospel. Later, when the bishop recognised the usefulness of my work, I was given an official mission.

Since then, I have almost always been in contact with students, whether they come from University Technical Institutes (IUT), Grandes Écoles or universities, in a variety of disciplines. Having learnt to combine my studies with my work, I have been involved in a multitude of groups and initiatives, such as the Service Incroyance et Foi (SIF, Faith and Faithlessness Service) and the Équipes de Dirigeants Chrétiens (EDC, Christian Management Teams). I have also taken part in a wide range of meetings, from team-building seminars for companies to interfaith meetings.

The Order encourages itinerant preaching, and my ideal is that of a seafaring preacher, a *marinero de muchas aguas*, a sailor navigating many seas, avoiding convinced circles as much as possible, shunning ecclesiastical structures and preferring to sail the frontiers[72]. I like to reinvent myself by leaving my comfort zone

---

[72] The General Chapter in Avila had a very fine chapter on being present on the frontiers of life and death, faith and atheism, marginalised social worlds, etc.

> **Faith in what? In whom?**
>
> There are several stages in the discovery of the Christian God. The first is curiosity, an initial interest. Régis Debray summed it up well when he said: *I am an unbeliever who is convinced that you have to believe.* In the Muslim world, all you have to do to affirm your faith is pronounce the *Shahada*[73].
>
> On the other hand, to be a Christian, reciting the creed is not enough. Debray implies that there is something missing to take the plunge. This *something* takes the form of an encounter, an experience, and constitutes the second stage. The conversion of Saint Paul is an emblematic reference.
>
> On the road to Damascus, he asked this fundamental question: *Who art Thou, Lord?* This question opens the way to the third stage, that of understanding faith. Deepening this faith then leads to theology, which becomes the intellectual exploration of this spiritual encounter.
>
> It is not enough to say that we have faith. You have to specify in what, or in whom, this faith is based, how it begins and how it evolves, what is essential and what is not. When I became a Brother Preacher, I had to study not agronomy or even theology, but philosophy[74], which provides the intellectual tools to express faith rationally. It allows us to dialogue with thinkers from different eras.
>
> Theology is nourished by these philosophical exchanges. Assimilating the great Tradition[75] takes time, and involves familiarising oneself with the reference authors: the Greek Fathers, such as Ignatius of Antioch, Gregory of Nyssa, Basil of Caesarea, Gregory of Nazianzus; the Latin Fathers, such as Augustine, Bernard and Thomas Aquinas; not forgetting, of course, contemporary theologians. Like Pentecost, no culture is superfluous when it comes to singing the wonders of God.

When computer use started becoming widespread, the region of Toulouse created a computer group, made up of Brother Hervé Ponsot and myself. With the help of a friend from Marseille, I set up

---

[73] *There is no god but God. Muhammad is the messenger of God.*

[74] At the University of Montpellier Paul Valéry, I was lucky enough, among other things, to take classes with Michel Henry, a phenomenologist who later confessed the Christian faith and supervised my master's thesis.

[75] Yves Congar O.P. wrote *La Tradition et les traditions* (Tradition and Traditions), in which he distinguishes Tradition, the creative sap animated by faith, from "traditions" that repeat themselves in a formalism without soul or creativity.

a Minitel service, allowing each convent to showcase its activities and provide dates and times.

I still remember my first Amstrad. It worked with floppy disks and had no hard disk. You had to insert the floppy disk containing the software (Wordstar, for those who remember these fossils), then another floppy disk to save your work. Could I have imagined where all this would lead?

Following a visit to the French sisters in Chiclayo[76] and the French brothers in Cusco[77] in Peru, I wrote a report for the *Concorde* bulletin, at the request of the provincial. I typed with my ten fingers, without looking at the keyboard, and I will never forget a sentence that was written as if mechanically. On the screen of my first computer, it appeared like a challenge: *If I were asked to go, I would not say no.* These words struck me as if they had been written by someone else. With this sentence, I simply wanted to express my solidarity with a community of French brothers whom I admired.

However, these words immediately seemed dangerous to me. In fact, a few years later, Brother Pierre Abeberry, then provincial, asked me delicately if I had changed my mind or if that statement still stood. I maintained my position... and left for Peru on 3 April 1992[78].

The change was so radical that an image came to mind, common in the Spanish-speaking world: *He vuelto a nacer* – a second birth in a totally new universe. This world was marked by the Spanish language and Quechua, work in difficult professional conditions, the omnipresent misery, and the civil war of *Sendero Luminoso*.

It was also the world of NGOs and solidarity. As the Gospel says: *[...] unless a grain of wheat fall into the ground and die, it abideth alone; but if it die, it bringeth forth much fruit.* I experienced this transformation, going through the discomfort of decomposition and recomposition – a kind of little death followed by resurrection.

---

[76] The Congregation of the Dominican Sisters of Albi. Sister Jacqueline in particular.

[77] Jean-Baptiste Lassègue, Guy Delran, Jean Max Hugues, Bernard Fulcrand, with a Portuguese friar, Henrique Urbano. Daniel Gilbert was staying in Lima.

[78] It was the fifth centenary of the discovery of the New World.

THE GENESIS OF THE INSTITUTION (1997-2005)

After spending several months working as an agricultural technician in high-altitude communities, I was appointed Director of the Bartolomé de las Casas Centre (CBC), an NGO specialising in action research. I soon became involved in issues relating to higher education.

Furthermore, I witnessed the emergence of the internet. Ironically, new technologies were developing faster there than in Europe. For example, installing mobile phone aerials was much cheaper than planting poles and laying cables. Under my direction, the CBC hired computer engineers who, in collaboration with the public university, installed the Internet node for the city of Cusco. The antenna stood proudly in a small patio.

One of the key players was Christine Goutet, a Franco-Peruvian who was a professor of IT at UNSAAC[79], the public university. She supported the NGOs, in particular with an accounting software package that she had designed. Percy Moya, head of the CBC's IT programme, has developed a series of websites for various regional institutions.

Thanks to him, we have discovered the use of email, which has revolutionised the way we work. Situated more than 300 km from another similar city, on a bad track crossing passes at an altitude of more than 4,000 metres, we were out of sight, out of mind. But with the Internet, geographical exclusion faded away, there were no more *peripheries*; we were all at the centre of the *global village*.

I had made the effort to inculturate myself in Peru, learning not only Spanish but also Quechua, immersing myself in the local literature and trying to understand the country's culture and history. I imagined staying there forever[80]. However, after being a delegate to the chapter in Toulouse, still feeling the effects of jet lag, I was elected provincial. I then had to organise my succession to the CBC. Fortunately, the vice-director, Yvonne Belaunde, a Peruvian

---

[79] National University of Saint Anthony the Abbot in Cusco (UNSAAC).

[80] See Michel Van Aerde, *L'Intime et le lointain* (The Intimate and the Distant), published by La Thune, Marseille, 2005.

laywoman, had all the qualities needed to take over. Thanks to her, the transition went naturally.

As all the missionaries say, coming back is much more difficult than leaving. Long gone is the excitement of discovery, even if the country of origin has changed. Fortunately, my new position offered me opportunities to travel, from Bordeaux to Nice, via Haiti and Madagascar, while at the same time allowing me to join a new network. At the invitation of Yvon Pomerleau[81] and Roger Houngbédji[82], assistants to the Master of the Order, I left for Rwanda, Burundi, Kenya, Madagascar, Mauritius, Reunion and South Africa.

After completing my term of office, I was appointed Promoter of Dominican Volunteers, which took me to the Philippines, Ecuador and across Europe. Then, as part of the international community in Brussels, where I was elected director of Espaces, my travels again took me to Ireland, Poland, Portugal, Italy, Hungary and as far afield as Turkey.

Then I was elected Vicar General of South Belgium, which led me to work on the union of the French-speaking and Dutch-speaking Dominican entities. These responsibilities, both regional and international, have only strengthened the network which, like a system of deep roots, has nourished our project.

As I contemplate my past, I see it as a series of successive lives, truly unpredictable[83], but which, with hindsight, reveal a profound coherence.

---

[81] Who had lived in Rwanda for a long time. He was then twice elected Provincial of Canada and President of the Conference of Major Superiors of his country.

[82] He has since been ordained Archbishop of Cotonou.

[83] My first book is *Quand Dieu nous surprend* (When God Surprises Us), La Thune, Marseille, 2000.

THE GENESIS OF THE INSTITUTION (1997-2005)

> **Planning or adhocracy?**
>
> Mi formación en biología me llevó a analizar la evolución del Centro Bartolomé de Las Casas, y luego de Domuni, de forma similar a la descrita por el Premio Nobel François Jacob en *La logique du vivant*. En él, compara la evolución con un inmenso bricolaje: una pata se convierte en un ala, una aleta o incluso una mandíbula... y todo cambia constantemente. Del mismo modo, un proyecto se convierte en un programa, luego se divide en varios departamentos bajo una dirección común, y así sucesivamente. Pero hay que distinguir entre el crecimiento, que es lineal y homogéneo, y el desarrollo, que implica etapas cualitativamente muy diferentes: crecimiento vegetativo, floración, fructificación y, por último, germinación.
>
> En cualquier proyecto empresarial, es crucial identificar estas fases, separadas por saltos cualitativos, ya sean técnicos, organizativos o de comunicación. Nuestra empresa ha experimentado metamorfosis similares a las de los batracios, las cigarras o las mariposas. Pero hay una diferencia fundamental: el desarrollo de un animal o una planta está inscrito en sus cromosomas, programado por su ADN. Para una empresa, en cambio, no existe un plan preestablecido que guíe su desarrollo. Cada decisión se toma dentro de una dinámica en la que el azar, la intuición y la libertad se entrelazan constantemente.
>
> Mi estilo de gestión se ha descrito como *ad-hocrático*, es decir, flexible e improvisado en función de las oportunidades que surgen. Sé a dónde quiero ir, pero no creo en planes rígidos a cinco o diez años. Es cierto que esto puede ser útil para las grandes empresas, donde una idea de la cúpula puede tardar años en llegar a la base. Pero en una institución pequeña, la inercia es casi inexistente. Las condiciones cambian constantemente, y es preferible aprovechar las oportunidades cuando son favorables, o virar para seguir avanzando cuando el viento sopla en contra.
>
> Nunca me he sentido tan aburrido como en las interminables reuniones de planificación de las ONG que he visitado. Tampoco he disfrutado en las sesiones de evaluación en las que acabas evaluando la propia evaluación. Tal y como yo lo veo, lo único que se necesita es una dirección clara, una definición de los objetivos prioritarios y evitar cualquier voluntarismo tenso.

There is one aspect of this picture that some may find irritating, and that is the question of gender relations. It is often overlooked when the Order of Preachers is mentioned, as if this universe were a world apart, populated by asexual beings, immune to the gender dynamics present in the rest of society.

> **A three-dimensional order**
>
> Históricamente, Domingo de Guzman fundó una pequeña comunidad diversificada en Fanjeaux, cerca de Carcasona, en el corazón del país cátaro. Esta comunidad estaba formada por algunas mujeres convertidas del catarismo, que se organizaron en un monasterio contemplativo, según el modelo de la época. También reunía a algunos sacerdotes, que más tarde se convertirían en frailes predicadores, así como a parejas de laicos, entre ellos Sanche y Godoline Gasc, prototipos de los futuros laicos dominicos. A diferencia de los franciscanos, que estaban organizados en tres órdenes independientes, los Predicadores formaban una sola orden compuesta por tres ramas distintas. Domingo presentó este grupo al obispo, llamándolo *La Santa Predicación*. Era, en cierto modo, una pequeña Iglesia en acción, dando testimonio, viviendo y predicando en un mundo postcristiano, no muy distinto del que vivimos hoy.
>
> Al principio, esta diversidad de carismas -los de los laicos, las religiosas y los religiosos- interactuaba en armonía. Con el tiempo, sin embargo, estas tres dimensiones se desarrollaron por separado, erosionando la sinergia que existía al principio. Hablar de *familia dominicana* como lo hacemos hoy no basta para ser fieles a la visión del fundador.

After I left the convent in Montpellier, I discovered another dimension of community life when I joined the small community in Cusco. Made up of a handful of friars, often on the move in the Andes or in Lima, this community had a house on Saphi Street in Cusco and maintained more or less close links with sisters, Dominican or not, as well as with lay people. Some of these sisters held positions of great responsibility. Eli Selem was administrator of the CBC. Sister Rosario Valdevellano, from the Congregation of the Sacred Heart, managed an impressive stock of food supplies sent by foreign countries to help the disaster-stricken population of the Inka region, an immense area equivalent to a quarter of France. The stock was like a cathedral, a huge warehouse filled with barrels of oil, sugar and flour, from which lorries left for the villages and communities...

With the civil war in Sendero Luminoso, the street where we lived in Cusco was far from safe. At night, soldiers from the barracks 300 metres down the road would sometimes panic, shooting at moonlight, thinking they saw enemies. In the morning, the telephone line was cut. To be on the safe side, Rosario would call us before leaving her office in her little Beetle. We waited for her at home, ready to open the gate as soon as she arrived, letting her car into the courtyard before closing the door as quickly as possible. These precautions were obviously paltry, as the door was made of light wood and the walls were easy to climb, but they reassured us nonetheless. We lived intensely, forming a group where the balance of charisms helped us to hold together, psychologically and spiritually. It was vital support at a time when police stations were being attacked, teachers had been murdered in the UNSAAC staff room where Christine Goutet taught, and a bomb had exploded just outside my office, just a month before I arrived. Could we have managed on our own, scattered in small groups of three or four brothers or sisters in different places? This community synergy, this concrete solidarity, was essential if we were to resist[84].

I had a similar experience in Haiti, in Pierre Payen, not far from the town of Saint Marc. There, the brothers preached with commitment, and were among the country's influential intellectuals. Godoline, a Flemish sister, ran a health clinic, mainly for children. Sister Elisabeth Tafel was involved in higher education, while sister Véronique Daquin, accompanied by another sister, had built a primary school and looked after the *restavek*, child servants reduced to the status of virtual slaves. The Dominican community was truly the beating heart of the valley, and entire lives depended on its actions. If love of neighbour or solidarity were preached, the words held actual weight.

When the sisters, too old to continue, had to return to Europe, the community's fragile balance collapsed. The social services provided by this group were no longer visible, and the disparity between the brothers' house, with its well-kept garden and cars, and the modest huts of the local inhabitants became glaring. This inequality fuelled the jealousy of the village's youth. Thefts began to occur: solar panels and vehicles were stolen. Then, when violence took over the country, the community, which had once been

---

[84] Ecclesiastes 4:12: *And if one prevail against him, two shall withstand him; and a threestrand cord is not quickly broken.*

respected and protected, no longer enjoyed the population's support. There was only one option left: to leave.

From these two experiences in extreme situations, where the combined efforts of three friars, three sisters and three lay people produced far superior results to those achieved by nine friars, nine sisters and nine lay people working separately, I realised from the outset that the development of Domuni could only take place if all the charisms resonated in harmony. The sisters, lay people and religious, united in this *Holy Preaching* and embodying *Dominic before the Dominicans*, had to join forces to strengthen the project.

> **Faith is born of preaching[85]; it cannot be taught**
>
> El lema de la Orden, *Veritas*, llama a predicar y enseñar, dos actividades que, aunque complementarias, son profundamente distintas. La fe no se puede enseñar, hay que proclamarla y proponerla, pero no se puede transmitir como una asignatura académica. Predicar no es dar explicaciones ni impartir conocimientos teóricos. Se trata más bien de dar testimonio, de abrir los ojos, de estimular el corazón, de liberar los oídos, de dar movimiento a los que están paralizados, de manifestar una alegría profunda y una vida insospechada. La fe no se comunica como un manojo de llaves, sino como el fuego. Si la fe pudiera transmitirse enseñando, entonces Jesús, tan incomprendido, podría ser calificado de mal maestro. Sin embargo, sabemos que fue un maestro excepcional. No daba respuestas prefabricadas, ni imponía dogmas; hacía preguntas. Con sus posturas desconcertantes, incitaba al cuestionamiento, llegando a preguntar *Para ti, ¿quién soy yo?* Y escuchaba.
>
> No, la fe no se puede enseñar. En cambio, cuando alguien llega a la fe, es bueno que pueda hacerla suya a través del testimonio y la reflexión de quienes le han precedido. Nuestra institución, aparte de algunos posts colocados aquí y allá en los recursos en línea, no tiene vocación de predicar el kerygma. Su misión consiste en transmitir la comprensión de la fe, es decir, en enseñar teología y otras disciplinas afines, que no están desprovistas de una teología implícita, y con las que la teología erudita puede debatir ventajosamente.

---

[85] Rm 10:17.

Should it be an association or a company?

Like a ship in peril facing reefs, our project nearly collapsed when our first employee took us to court. This ordeal left me deeply psychologically exhausted and destabilised me. As chairman of the association, I asked myself: had I become an employer, an irresponsible boss, or worse, an exploiter?

The governance of an association under the law of 1901 is subject to the principles of democracy, with the chairman having limited discretion in decision-making. They have to inform, explain, and, above all, reassure associate members, who are all volunteers with no desire to be involved in a conflict. This discomfort is even more pronounced in a religious association. Called to bear witness to God's love, they hope to be loved in return. Although they have chosen poverty and uncertain material circumstances, they have set themselves the ambitious goals they are known for throughout history: teaching, promoting health, defending the weak, and demanding justice. They are accustomed to receiving support from the laity.

Following the trauma of the separation of church and state, the confiscation of church property, and their subsequent expulsion, these religious groups fear nothing more than having to face the public authorities again.

> **Suppressed three times, resurrected three times**
>
> Due to their democratic organisation and international outlook, the Dominicans have always been viewed with suspicion by those in power, ever since the Ancien Régime. As in many other countries, they were suppressed several times in France. The first time they were abolished was in 1790, shortly after the French Revolution. However, Henri Lacordaire reestablished them in 1843. They were suppressed again in September 1870, after which the expelled Dominicans found refuge in neighbouring countries[86].
>
> Finally, in 1902, they suffered another expulsion, followed by the confiscation of their property in 1905.
>
> It was only after the First World War, during which the Dominicans had shared the common fate of the trenches, that they began to secretly resettle in France[87]. Not owning their own homes, they hid under the guise of various secular associations, such as the Association de l'Étoile and the Association de l'Esplanade. They lived in a veritable jungle of associations, as complex and obscure as possible. It was only after President Giscard d'Estaing signed an international treaty in Finland that they realised they were no longer at risk of religious persecution. I was already among them at that time!
>
> From then on, the Dominicans started creating their own associations under their real names, such as the "Dominican Province of France" or the "Convent of the Dominicans of such-and-such a town". After ascertaining that there would be no negative repercussions, they began to invest in some real estate under these associations. Thus, having previously been dependent minors, subject to the goodwill of lay people acting as nominees, they once again became masters of their own rights. This history explains their continued reserve towards public authorities. A hearing at an industrial tribunal involving a religious association can therefore feel like a tsunami in a font.

A., hired as an IT specialist, administered his domain with total autonomy and did not reveal how he had structured it. We placed blind trust in him until Françoise and Dominique Michel made a disturbing revelation: there were in fact two separate sites. The public

---

[86] "D'expulsion en expulsion, les dominicains de la province d'Occitanie en Valais" (From expulsion to expulsion, the Dominicans of the province of Occitania in Valais). Brother Bernard Hodel, O.P., *Academia*, 1997.

[87] The Dominicans were a dissolved association, and therefore banned.

site was accessible to everyone, while the Dokeos open access teaching platform hosted the courses.

Only after this conflict did we regain control of the IT infrastructure and realise the urgent need to clarify who was making the decisions. We had to implement proper management procedures. Until then, we had so much confidence in A.'s technical abilities that we were willing to delegate most practical decisions to him. As well as the technical management for which he had been hired, he also managed the administration and student follow-up. We had even considered appointing him director of the programme. We naively believed that by giving him this title, *ex opere operato*, he would be given the skills and vision that go with it. The subsequent conflicts saved us from making this mistake.

As soon as it became necessary to obtain resources from the beneficiaries to pay the facilitator, our little institution could no longer operate as a simple voluntary association. We were entering the realm of business logic, which required rigorous management. In contemporary terms, we needed a real manager. At the time, we were not aware of this, but each subsequent conflict would help us to recognise it. Each challenge we faced gave us a better understanding of the inevitable cultural change required. Transforming a voluntary association into a company was no easy task. Linking this new structure to a traditionally risk-averse Order was no easy task either.

It became crucial to redefine roles and clarify access to IT systems. Following the Aristotelian principle of the priority of the final cause, it was imperative that pedagogical direction drove technical developments, rather than the other way around. Pedagogy had to remain in control, with technology at its service. Even if they were not computer experts, the teachers had to be able to manage changes to the web pages, just as a driver manages their car without needing to consult the garage more than once a year. Brother Bruno Cadoré pointed out that computer scientists often have a tendency to monopolise power by interfering in decisions that are outside their area of expertise. He gave the striking example of his time as a professor of medicine, when technicians in operating theatres came into conflict with surgeons over issues outside their remit.

This realisation marked a decisive turning point. In order to ensure that the educational purpose remained at the heart of our actions, we needed to select computer programmes that were straightforward enough for teachers to use independently. On several occasions, we found that our university partners were paralysed by technical obstacles, which compromised their ability to evolve. By freeing teaching from technological constraints, we have fostered creativity.

On 8 March 2012, the Toulouse Court of Appeal issued the following ruling:

> *The Court confirmed the decision of the Toulouse industrial tribunal in all its provisions, adding:*
>
> *Each party shall bear the costs and expenses incurred before the Court.*

This was a great relief. The dispute with our first employee lasted from January 2008 to March 2012 – more than four exhausting, dangerous, yet instructive years. Faced with this experience, our association made some pragmatic decisions.

As the general management was based in Belgium, we chose to hire the next employees there, taking advantage of employment laws based on a different philosophy. This system offered employees benefits such as a thirteenth month's pay and even a fourteenth month's pay in the form of a *holiday pay*, indexed to inflation. Conversely, there was notable contractual flexibility: fixed-term and open-ended contracts were indistinguishable, and termination of a contract simply involved paying the statutory indemnities.

Institutional and academic development

What was the founding moment of our institution? On 23 November 1998, the two Provincial Councils of the French Dominican Provinces met exceptionally at the convent in Toulouse, as the minutes indicate:

> *Despite the rail strike, councillors from France and Toulouse gathered at the convent in Rangueil for the joint meeting of the two Provincial Councils. A large part of the meeting was*

devoted to examining the principles, statutes and provisional budget of the proposed association: Domuni...

The two provinces undertake to support the project financially and to each appoint a promoter for the DOMUNI project. They also undertake to continue reflecting on the academic and institutional aspects of the project with a view to compiling an academic application and obtaining canonical recognition.

Since its publication in the *Journal Officiel* on 13 February 1999, the establishment's legal status has been that of a not-for-profit association under the 1901 law. Br Hervé Ponsot had wanted it to be controlled by the Dominicans. As they made up 100% of the General Assembly, there were no women, and six members of the Board of Directors were appointed by right: the two provincials, the two regents of studies and the two provincial librarians.

In theory, the model seemed well conceived. In practice, however, it left much to be desired. For example, the librarians were constantly absent, and their role was subsequently removed. As Brother Bruno Cadoré noted with compassion, *there were those who swam in the pool and those who watched*. The vast majority of the association's members were not actively involved in the day-to-day running of the university. Many had never taught a course, led a seminar, met a student, graded a paper or supervised an exam. They might have browsed the public site once, but they had never accessed the teaching platform.

When a member by right exclaimed, *I do not understand anything*, nobody encouraged them to make an effort, to get informed, or to delegate to someone competent. I had to put up with this irresponsibility for twenty-five years, and I doubt that my successors will be able to tolerate the same discomfort. The lesson to be learnt is clear: the members of the General Meeting and the Board of Directors must be selected from among people who are informed and involved, who have mastered the new technologies and understand the realities at stake in the debates.

> **The conditions for fraternity**
>
> The soul of the Order of Preachers is rooted in a historic act. During the first General Chapter of 1220 in Bologna, Saint Dominic, papal legate and founder, resigned. He wanted his authority to come not from above, but from below, from the friars themselves. This radical reversal was a manifestation of a theology of the Spirit, capable of inspiring a true ecclesiology, a form of *"philadelphia"*, or brotherly love.

The statutes of the association, those of the Academic Council, and the various regulations and procedures form the soul, the structure, the DNA of our institution. However, they reveal an implicit theology, of which we are trying to become fully aware. Affirming the primacy of democracy and ensuring the balanced representation of the three bodies – the student body, the teaching body and the administrative, pedagogical and technical body – promotes a theology of fraternity, dialogue and freedom.

Adhering to the procedures for electing the rector while honouring the democratic spirit is part of a genuine pneumatology – a theology of the Spirit. From this perspective, truth does not emanate from on high. As Thomas Aquinas said, the argument from authority is one of the weakest. This model eliminates the need for a "father", a "major superior" or a protective bishop, instead relying on collective trust and a shared quest for truth nourished by open-mindedness and fraternal dynamics.

Our establishment has a complete institutional structure as a multilingual university, ensuring democratic operation in full harmony with that of the Order of Preachers. The legal personality is carried by the French association, recognised by the French State. It includes members from different countries. The Academic Senate, a true legislative body, governs the core of academic operations, while the Rectorate is responsible for the executive, reporting to both the Senate and the association.

As a not-for-profit association, profits cannot be redistributed to members, but are reinvested in activities or directed to organisations with similar objectives. In France, non-profit status means that donations can be issued with tax receipts. Obtaining this recognition required complex procedures, in particular with the help of a tax lawyer. Little by little, all these steps helped to consolidate the institution. The official letter from the Public Finances, dated 28 January 2014, is worth quoting here, as it describes precisely the nature and missions of our establishment.

> *The association's purpose is to provide higher education in theology, philosophy and religious sciences at university level. It offers trilingual online training with ongoing support from a personal tutor and an active international student community.*
>
> *On 29 March 2011, the association declared the opening of a private higher education course to the Academy of Toulouse Rectorate.*
>
> *In addition, on 25 April 2013, it signed a cooperation agreement with the University of Lorraine to ensure teaching equivalence between the two institutions and enable DOMUNI students to obtain state-recognised diplomas awarded by the University of Lorraine.*
>
> *It should be noted that the organisation is not for profit, and its directors and teachers are all volunteers.*
>
> *It provides higher education to students regardless of their geographical location, origin, opinions or beliefs.*
>
> *It does not operate on a competitive field, bearing in mind that access to training can be free for underprivileged people...*

Based on the French association's model, two other associations have been set up: the International Non-Profit Association (AISBL) Domuni Europe, based in Brussels, and Domuni Suisse, based in Geneva. The purpose of these bodies was to manage employees in their respective countries. Despite the strides made by the European Union, employing a British employee on a part-time basis in Brussels offices, under the aegis of a French association, proved practically unfeasible.

Setting up a relay association was a simpler and less costly solution. These three associations, which have the same objectives, have an agreement that their aims converge in the activities of the university, under the direction of the rector.

Consolidated accounts, pooling the financial results of the three associations, are presented each year to provide a clear overview of the institution's overall financial situation.

In 2010, the Congregation for Catholic Education (CCE) established the Higher Institute for Religious Sciences (HIRS) and recognised its affiliation[88] with the Angelicum. The statutes approved by the Holy See at this time provided a framework for the institution. However, these statutes were soon found to be too restrictive for the subsequent development of the Faculty of Theology and, even more so, for the establishment of two new faculties: the Faculty of Philosophy and the Faculty of Humanities and Social Sciences.

Preparing an application for the Swiss Agency for Quality and Accreditation (AAQ) to obtain institutional accreditation required new statutes, regulations and procedures to be created. A committee led by Marie Monnet, with the participation of Brother Guido Vergauwen (former rector of the University of Fribourg), worked on drafting the Academic Senate's statutes. These statutes were then ratified by a vote of the association. The Academic Senate, comprising equal numbers from the three university bodies and the three associations, acts as a parliament and embodies the institution's legislative power.

It was able to debate and vote on the various regulations and statutes of the faculties and academic bodies[89], while also drawing up the procedures for electing the rector. These procedures were then ratified by the Board of Directors of the French association. The Senate meets twice a year to receive the rector's annual report. It also acts as an appeals body in the event of a conflict, and can arbitrate if a sanction decided by a faculty council is contested, for example[90].

The statutes of each faculty specify the composition of its board, the method of appointment, the dean's duties and the

---

[88] On 24 March 2010, the Domuni-Angelicum agreement was signed by Brother Charles Morerod, Rector of the Angelicum, and Brother Michel Van Aerde, Director General of Domuni.

[89] There are three academic bodies: teaching staff, students, and administrative, technical and teaching staff.

[90] In the case of plagiarism, for example, which unfortunately is not uncommon, or a student insulting a teacher, which fortunately is not common, the Senate can intervene.

procedures for integrating new lecturers, welcoming new courses and defining research themes.

Just as the human body continually renews itself with new cells while retaining its identity, a university maintains its coherence through its statutes despite the constant renewal of its students, teaching and administrative staff. The quality system involves everyone and aims to move the whole institution forward. While the individual contributions of teachers and members of the Rectorate are important, it is the statutes and regulations that provide the underlying structure. These statutes and regulations are the very soul of Domuni, in harmony with its founding intuitions, vision and mission.

Financing, both ordinary and extraordinary

Although the Friar Preachers no longer roam the streets begging for bread, their vocation as beggars remains in their DNA, following the example of the Carmelites and Franciscans. Poverty remains an essential dimension of their preaching. *Go, without taking either... or... and preach, saying, "The Kingdom of Heaven is at hand".* Those who have experienced the joy of spontaneous hospitality as a result of an accident or misadventure have lived this fulfilled utopia, this anticipation of eschatology.

It is an experience of the Kingdom in action for both those who welcome and those who are welcomed, *for the people of the streets as for the people of the houses*, as Madeleine Delbrel used to say. Jesus does not specify the message to be conveyed, but insists on the experience to be had. The disciples were sent out two by two to live in fraternity and friendship if possible, in order to offer a shared message and a living word.

Volunteering was therefore the norm in the early days. Brother Hervé Ponsot would have liked everything to be offered free of charge, like Google or Wikipedia. He based his work on the evangelical injunction to give freely what one has received freely. The teachers were not paid for submitting their manuscripts, but received generous compensation for each copy corrected, each seminar led and each dissertation directed. Personally, I was not in favour of completely free tuition. My experience working for an NGO in Peru had shown me the importance of involving the beneficiaries, even symbolically. It gave them rights and turned them into responsible players, committed supporters of the activity, rather than mere recipients.

In 2003, while I was spending several months in Haiti, it became clear that we would not be able to meet the salary of A., our sole employee and main source of expenditure. Faced with this critical situation, I appealed to my friends and my sister Véronique. Their generous response enabled us to overcome this immediate difficulty, but it was clear that this one-off help was not a permanent solution.

So I insisted on the need to set up online payment and make registration more accessible. I explained to A. that, in order to pay him, we had to generate revenue, and that this revenue had to come from the beneficiaries themselves. I tried to explain it to him, saying *it is a system of communicating vessels: if one tap empties the basin, another has to fill it up.*

For several years, the two French provinces and the General Curia of the Order fully covered the costs. This can be seen in the financial accounts for this period. As with the Centro Bartolomé de Las Casas (CBC) in Cusco, the running of our establishment could not rely entirely on donations from charitable agencies.

At the time, I initiated a policy of self-financing at the CBC, an approach that was quickly emulated by most NGOs. For Domuni, the principle was clear: operating costs had to be covered by income, while the search for donations had to focus on grants and the necessary investments.

The two main objectives were to ensure financial equilibrium by increasing income from enrolments and to find sponsors to finance long-term investments. Thanks to Marie Monnet's determined efforts, we were able to implement a sustainable economic model. By adopting the recently set Bologna standards for universities and adjusting fees to a realistic level, student contributions have gradually enabled the institution to stop burdening the French provinces.

Marie Monnet also considerably simplified the enrolment process by introducing the Moodle teaching platform to replace the old Dokeos system. This modernisation was part of an ongoing effort to streamline operations.

At a meeting of the Board of Directors, Brother Jean-Hugo Tisin, who was Regent of Studies at the time, revealed that we were asking our students to complete three times the amount of homework and exams required of a full-time Dominican student. Were we suffering from an inferiority complex in relation to face-to-face courses?

To remedy this, we decided to reduce the number of courses, assignments and exams, and to adhere to university standards. Courses have been enriched and consolidated, often increasing from three ECTS credits to six, with one assignment per course. As a result, the number of assignments has been reduced to ten per academic year, making the workload heavy but reasonable. Drop-out rates after the first year fell considerably, re-enrolments increased, and grading costs per year were halved.

Each semester concluded with a written examination session invigilated at an approved institutional centre. The papers were scanned and sent to graders wherever they were located. This method minimised transport costs, a trend that was further reinforced by the adoption of Zoom oral examinations, which became commonplace in universities around the world in the wake of the Covid-19 pandemic.

With the emergence of artificial intelligence tools, it had become impossible for the Plagium software to detect a new form of plagiarism. In fact, each answer generated by ChatGPT to a single question was unique. To overcome this challenge, it was agreed that students would be subject to a live oral examination, strengthening the pedagogical relationship between teachers and students.

Investments took various forms, including the creation of new courses and the translation of the website into several languages (French, English, Spanish, Italian and Arabic). New IT programmes were adopted to modernise the teaching platform and website and to develop administration tools for managing student data, files, grades and diplomas. These efforts were accompanied by institutional consolidation in the form of regulations, statutes and accounting, as well as the creation of associations in Belgium and Switzerland, and the signing of agreements with various university partners, including

Angelicum, University of Lorraine, University of Louvain, Priory Institute, Escuela de Teologia de Salamanca, and Bagdad Academy. Additionally, establishing the Domuni-Press university publishing house marked a new stage in our institution's development.

As director of the CBC in Cusco, I had become accustomed to fundraising on an international scale – invaluable experience when I was elected head of the Dominicans in French-speaking Belgium. This led me to seek funds for two major projects: the construction of the convent in Louvain-la-Neuve, and the restoration of the church and organ in the convent in Brussels. Although the Belgian Vicariate General's finances were in balance, they did not allow for such investments. F. was sympathetic to the projects, however, and offered to make a donation. I therefore drew up a detailed document using Google Earth images to show that, although the Brussels convent was further away than the neighbouring mosque, it was just a few hundred metres from the offices of the European Commission. In addition to the many private donations, Total and the Chimay monastery, famous for its Trappist beers, also contributed.

Is modern fundraising a contemporary version of medieval begging? I would not go that far, but there are similarities. The project always takes precedence over the means; you do not wait for the means to come together before you start.

Once the convent in Louvain-la-Neuve had been completed, we organised a gathering of patrons in the presence of Br Bruno Cadoré, Master of the Order, who paid us a fraternal visit. Speeches of thanks were given, followed by a toast to celebrate the achievement of these projects.

After the ceremony, during informal discussions, F. asked a key question: did we have any other projects that would need financial support? I introduced him to Br Patrick Gillard, whose remarkable work in helping prostitutes out of their condition deserved support, and we also discussed the work of Domuni.

The concept of this university immediately appealed to him. We arranged a meeting. An intuitive businessman, F. had already seen the opportunity of online higher education and had sent me some insightful articles, mainly American, on the evolution of universities around the world. I was able to present to him our wish to develop teaching in English, in collaboration with the Dominicans of Oxford and Cambridge, the Priory Institute in Ireland, and the English section of the Angelicum. *How much do you need?* He asked. I replied that the salary of an English theologian for one year was €70,000. This was a negligible sum compared to what he had already committed to the Catholic University of Louvain, of which he was a major patron. He replied: *I will give you €100,000*. The very next day, the money was paid into the charity's account.

When it comes to fund-raising, several elements are crucial: the quality of the project, which must be in line with the interests of the donor; accountability, i.e. rigour in the execution of the project and transparency in the accounts; and lastly, trust, which is built up and strengthened over the years.

Jill Alexy, an American, was hired on the recommendation of Brother Charles Morerod, op, then rector of the Angelicum, who had met her among his students shortly before he became Bishop of Fribourg, Lausanne, Neuchâtel and Geneva. Jill moved to Brussels, and with Marie Monnet, we travelled to Dublin, Rome, Ottawa, Toronto, Cambridge and Oxford to collect the theology and philosophy courses needed to set up a bachelor's and master's degree in theology in English. Each stage was a real challenge, but we succeeded by convincing teachers, one by one, to join our project.

In 2013, we presented an ambitious three-year project, entitled *Metamorphosis*, to the Fondation X. This dense thirty-page document, written in English, clearly expressed our state of mind: *We will do it alone, but with your help we will be able to do it professionally and without burning out.* A decisive meeting took place in Brussels.

At the time, I was Vicar General of the French-speaking Belgian Dominicans. Jill arrived in my office, American style, with drinks and cakes, which pleasantly surprised C., the foundation's representative. We were able to explain our project to him in a fluid discussion, half in English, half in French, and he was very interested.

Then, unexpectedly, on our way out, we bumped into Brother Tam Nguyen, who is Vietnamese by birth. He ran over to C. and greeted him warmly. I then learned that the Fondation X. had financed his studies at Louvain. This same Brother Tam, who had become a doctor of theology, would soon be in charge of our English teaching. The stars were truly aligned for our project! The sponsors could see the multiplier effect of their donations.

Brother Tam was able to provide mentoring in English for several years, before being replaced by Brother Srecko Koralija, a Croatian, who had just successfully defended his doctorate at Cambridge. After the successful introduction of teaching in English, the Fondation X. continued to support our efforts, in particular by funding the introduction of courses in Italian and the development of online resources.

The next project, *Domuni Quality-PhD-Accreditations*, financed our work with the Swiss Agency of Accreditation and Quality Assurance (AAQ).

An ambitious project for 2023-2026 is currently underway: *DOMUNI in synergy with partner universities*. This project aims to strengthen the links between Domuni and its university partners, in order to create a genuine network of universities.

By pooling courses, teachers and services such as the Moodle platform, local tutoring and the organisation of examinations, each institution can offer courses that it would not be able to develop on its own. Training courses for administrative staff and research collaborations, such as co-publications and international colloquia, further strengthen this network.

Our institution's economic model is based on enrolment fees paid by students from the outset. However, operational costs, such as grading assignments, examinations and mentoring, are spread over the duration of their course. This means that solid financial reserves are needed to guarantee the continuity of the business in the long term.

Ideally, we should keep a year's cash in advance to ensure that students are secure throughout their studies. But inflation, which is eating away at the funds, complicates this prudent management. As the most beneficial investments are too hazardous, we must tread carefully through this economic uncertainty.

Brother Timothy Radcliffe[91] pointed out to me that many American universities have substantial endowments funded by donations from alumni and corporations.

These funds, invested on the stock exchange, sometimes generate more income than the registrations themselves. This raises the question of whether our institution should consider creating such a foundation one day. This would transform our relationship with students and how we operate on a daily basis.

The current model, which is based on limited resources and self-financing, leaves us in a precarious position – which in turn stimulates our adaptability and responsiveness. It forces us to be creative and constantly rethink our organisation and methods.

This uncertainty reflects a fundamental spiritual and theological question: I believe in the triumph of the love of a weak and poor God. This conviction anchors our mission in accepted fragility, where simplicity and trust take centre stage in our way of living and transmitting our values and faith, and where efficiency is not sought at any price.

---

[91] Elected Master of the Order in 1992, he was created Cardinal in October 2024, along with Brother Jean-Paul Vesco, former President of Domuni, who was later ordained Archbishop of Oran and then Algiers.

Taking off (2005-2020)

Marie Monnet, Dominican lawyer and theologian

Among those who have shaped the current face of Domuni Universitas, Marie Monnet occupies a unique place. Committed to the institution since 2007, she has accompanied all the stages of its structuring and growth, until her election, in May 2023, as the first elected rector.

From the outset, Marie Monnet has put her academic background - acquired at the Sorbonne, the Institut Catholique de Toulouse, the Catholic University of Louvain, the Angelicum, the IEP in Toulouse and the Ecole des Avocats de Paris - at the service of building a solid academic framework. At a time when the Bologna agreements had just been signed, he farsightedly pushed for the implementation of the Bachelor-Master-Doctorate system. While other institutions were slow to adapt, Domuni adapted in just a few weeks, offering structured training programmes in line with European standards.

In the same spirit of transformation, Marie Monnet proposed an evolution of the economic model: to move from symbolic contributions to an annual tuition fee aligned with the reality of the service provided. For her, the challenge was not financial, but profoundly cultural: to allow the university to ensure its autonomy, to preserve what constituted its wealth: the freedom to think, to teach and to undertake. She put it bluntly, with a hint of provocation: "We have to get out of this nun mentality, where one sacrifices oneself and everything must be free. What costs nothing is worth nothing". Far from being a retreat, this statement was intended to bring about the emergence of a culture of fair value, based on reciprocity and recognition of work done. The resulting change in approach enabled Domuni to consolidate its viability while remaining true to its mission.

Endowed with a keen sense of organisation, Marie Monnet encouraged the transition to efficient digital tools. She initiated the adoption of the Moodle platform, which she herself configured on the basis of online tutorials, in particular by automating enrolment for all the one-year courses. With this initiative and many others - generalisation of videoconferencing tools, redesign of interfaces, new ways of accompanying students - she opened the way to a pedagogy that was truly adapted to distance learning.

At the same time, Marie Monnet promoted the creation of Domuni-Press, a university publishing house for the publication of books with ISBN and journals with ISSN, disseminated through both traditional and digital channels. The aim: to promote the work of academics and provide scientific visibility on an international scale.

In the field of external relations, he played a decisive role in the development of partnerships and the organisation of congresses in various countries: in France, the Middle East, Latin America, Iraq, Africa and Salamanca. He also coordinated Domuni's application to the UN, obtaining for the university the status of NGO associated with the Economic and Social Council (Ecosoc). On that day in New York, his impromptu speech at the plenary assembly, in front of demanding diplomats, was able to convince and make people recognise the usefulness of a free academic actor, committed to the dialogue of cultures.

Behind the diversity of initiatives, the constancy of his commitment to others is impressive. Her energy never seems to be driven by the pursuit of personal interest, but by a keen awareness of a need, in the service of those she accompanies. In Marie Monnet there is a perseverance that is foolproof, a mysterious constancy that does not come, as it often does, from anger, but is lived day by day, step by step, as a necessity, an ongoing discovery, a renewed astonishment.

Hyperalert by nature, Marie Monnet always seems to be attentive to what can further the common mission. She lives and encourages a concrete and committed fraternity.

Her rigour did not prevent her from cultivating a contagious humour. When she allows herself a moment's rest, the atmosphere brightens up: the seriousness of her work gives way to sincere laughter, often provoked by her talents of imitation, of which everyone remembers some scenes that have become mythical. These moments reveal a lesser-known side of her: that of a woman inhabited by a great joie de vivre, despite the constant pressure.

Her academic background shows an uncommon tenacity: a degree in philosophy, a DEA in Louvain, a doctorate in theology, and then a full legal training up to the bar. The subjects he deals with - fundamental rights, freedom of movement, gender, the place of women in the Church - are sensitive. She deals with them with rigour and depth, true to her intuition that reflection can and must precede consensus.

Beyond her visible functions, Marie Monnet embodies a structuring, demanding and fruitful form of presence. Some wonder about her future: theatre, politics, cinema? What is certain is that she will continue to act whenever she perceives that a path may open up. Communicating life, remembering that joy is possible, and that the Kingdom is there to be welcomed here and now - this is what seems to animate Marie, in the shadow as well as in the light.

Ecclesiastical recognition

From 27 November 2007 onwards[92], successive meetings in Rome were superimposed on each other in my memory, like layers of puff pastry, always taking place in the same lounge in the offices of the Congregation for Catholic Education[93].

The interlocutors changed, but the atmosphere remained the same. There was a sense of eternity floating around those moments. We were in the heart of St Peter's Square, where the *Via della Conciliazione* begins.

As I was leaving Santa Sabina, Brother Bruno Cadoré, who was not yet Master of the Order, warned me: *Prophecy stops where*

---

[92] See my report in the archives.
[93] Today, the "Dicastery for Culture and Education".

diplomacy begins. And yet, faced with the incessant question: *By whom are you recognised?* Should we not have introduced ourselves?

The very first visit[94] was organised by Brother Marcio Couto, assistant to the Master of the Order for Intellectual Life, a charming Brazilian, a former student of Fribourg, who spoke excellent French. *They need to get to know you, he said, so that they are not afraid of you (!). We do not have any specific requests, just the wish to meet them. When you come back, they will remember you and it will be easier to talk to them.*

I then asked him: *what should we wear?* He replied that it would be better to dress like them because, if we wore the Dominican habit, the first ten minutes of the conversation would be spent discussing it, and we would lose precious time. He suggested I put on a Roman collar – he would lend me one. And so I did.

It was comical. Ten metres from the door, we adjusted the little white plastic bar on our collar, and as we descended the stairs, we immediately took it off. Marcio was very relaxed – par for the course for the Italians. There is a time for everything, for formality as well as spontaneity. And the visit, in this relaxed atmosphere, went well.

Mgr Z., the undersecretary of the Congregation, a French-speaking Italian, received us with almost excessive friendliness. *What you are doing is really good and very important. It is a great service. We are very grateful to you.* He kept telling us what a *wonderful experience* it had been and showered us with compliments. However, after all that praise came the relentless punchline: *But... it is blocked.*

Flabbergasted, I asked: *What do you mean, it is blocked? – Yes, it is blocked. Here, the Internet is seen as dangerous, because of the possibility of pornography. Cardinals obsess over this. They are even going to install filters to block certain sites...*

We had not expected anything more after the interview. We had received warm compliments and thanks. At that stage, we had no other ambitions. He said it was blocked... and yet, three months later,

---

[94] 27 Nov. 2007, see the report in the archives.

it was unblocked for a faculty in Barcelona, as I discovered online. The door was ajar. We just had to try.

So we went back to Rome to meet another undersecretary of the Congregation for Catholic Education and prepare a new application. On the advice of Brother Marcio Couto, we followed a simple strategy: copy the statutes of the HIRS *Mater Ecclesiae* of the Angelicum, recently erected and already approved. If that application had been accepted, why should not ours be too? It was not a question of rethinking what might suit us better, but pragmatically of reproducing a model that had already been validated. But our application was rejected, without the slightest encouragement to persevere. With determination, the comments were given full consideration and a second, improved application was submitted. Brother Joseph Van Than Tam, Dean of the Faculty of Theology at the Angelicum, helped me with this meticulous revision, examining it in great detail, down to every comma. I had never worked so hard. On the third attempt, led by the highly diplomatic Sister Marie Monnet, our application was approved. *An application is never accepted the first time*, explained Brother Joseph Agius, former rector and new dean.

> **The Vatican? An administration smaller than that of a French sub-prefecture**
>
> But did the disproportion between the mission and the means justify or excuse the mistreatment we experienced at the hands of the Holy See? When we visited the Congregation for Catholic Education, it had eight people, all in all. Eight people to manage Catholic universities and faculties all over the world, in every language! With so few human and material resources – did they even have at least one computer per office? – the method adopted was to appear more daunting an impenetrable than it really was.
>
> In hindsight, and putting aside our feelings in the matter, we should have been more understanding. The Roman staff needed to manage the Catholic Church as a whole was barely half the size of a large hospital. Two thousand five hundred people. A trifle, to be sure, but did they really need to be more numerous? It reminded me of Pope John XXIII's quip when asked how many people worked in the Vatican: *About half*, he replied.

After six years *ad experimentum*, on 19 January 2016, the Angelicum's Academic Council unanimously approved our self-evaluation at an extraordinary session attended by Marie Monnet and myself. However, the Congregation for Catholic Education refused the request for renewal. Mgr Z., in a meeting from which I was unusually excluded[95], explained to the provincials and to the president of the association, Brother Jean Claude Lavigne, that *the time of Bruguès was over*[96].

As we never received a reply from the Congregation to our last letter, we took a difficult but necessary decision: rather than scuttling ourselves, we chose to continue to grow without this canonical recognition. Teaching theology is not a crime, and if we want to reduce the clericalism that Pope Francis is always complaining about, should we not encourage lay people to train?

Since then, the Spanish provinces have gradually withdrawn. Yet was it not precisely this freedom of thought, enterprise and research that our institution was supposed to defend? Could we renounce it without betraying our vocation?

To my question *Do you give out canonical titles (recognised by the Catholic Church)?* The rector of a leading Jesuit university replied: *No, we want to remain free.* I wish that being Catholic and being free were not mutually exclusive!

A visit to Florence gave me a glimpse behind the scenes of this very special little world. C., encouraging me to meet the other institutions funded by the Fondation X., directed me to the Sophia University Institute, near Florence, where Monsignor D., its president, was rumoured to be a friend of Pope Francis and one of the authors of *Veritatis Gaudium*. This text is admirable, as we have already emphasised. The intuitions it conveys are powerful, but, alas, the implementing decrees go in the opposite direction. The rectors and deans I met confirmed that there are two antagonistic authors behind

---

[95] Yet it was specified in the Statutes of the HIRS Domuni, approved by the Congregation, that the Director General had to be present at all meetings concerning the HIRS. The Congregation for Catholic Education does not respect its own rules.

[96] Mgr Jean-Louis Bruguès, a friar of the Dominican province of Toulouse, of which he had been elected provincial, was then ordained Bishop of Angers and appointed secretary of the Congregation for Catholic Education. Succession troubles in this Roman institution?

Veritatis Gaudium. The unfortunate thing is that it is the decrees that prevail, rather than the vital impetus instilled by the main text.

Monsignor D. gave us such a warm welcome that we were almost taken aback. He showed us around his establishment, gave us a long audience in his office, listened attentively to my complaints about the Congregation, and promised me an informal meeting to clarify the situation. He then introduced us to his successor with a view to finalising a collaboration agreement. At the end, he invited us to pray together, giving thanks for our work, blessing our efforts and invoking the help of the Holy Spirit. With palpable emotion, he went so far as to ask for our forgiveness, in a gesture so sincere that it deeply moved me. It felt like inner therapy and a genuine liberation.

Nothing came of it and, for Domuni, nothing had changed. However, one question still lingers in my mind: why did Monsignor D. ask us to forgive him, and in whose name? How did he really see us? I sent him several emails, which went unanswered. Did he see us as innocent victims, crushed by a blind system that he knew all too well, but against which he could do nothing? Since that was the case, we had to take responsibility for ourselves. Were the days of Bruguès "over"? That of his successors would also pass.

Since I am talking about Rome and Italy, this is a good time to do justice to Brother Francesco Compagnoni, a Dominican a little older than me, who developed the teaching of Italian in our school.

I met Brother Francesco at the General Chapter of the Friars Preachers in Bologna in July 1998, and we hit it off immediately. At the time, he was Dean of the Faculty of Social Sciences (FASS) at the Pontifical University of Saint Thomas Aquinas (PUST) in Rome, better known as the Angelicum. Later, when he was elected rector, he invited me to introduce Domuni to the teaching staff, but to no avail. It was only after Domuni had received official recognition from the Holy See that we were able to sign the agreement linking the HIRS to the PUST Faculty of Theology.

Francesco, together with the Dean of FASS, Brother Alejandro Crosthwaite, proposed that we enter into a specific agreement for his faculty's university certificates in Italian, delivered via our platform.

He was instrumental in finding courses in English and Italian. I have always considered him a friend.

Rome is a fascinating city. Visiting with the aim of establishing an international university for the teaching of theology opens doors that ordinary tourists never pass through. To develop our English teaching, we met a young German priest who was already a Doctor of Theology and was staying at the Teutonic College, which is located just to the left as you enter the Vatican, on the way to St Martha's House, where Pope Francis lives. We did not try to disturb him, of course, but from the college's roof, our professor offered us a spectacular bird's-eye view of the world's smallest state.

Later, as he had some free time and was happy to help, I suggested we visit the catacombs located just below the dome of St Peter's Basilica. There, we were able to get very close to the famous yellow casket in which, according to archaeologists[97], the relics of Saint Peter are kept. We prayed sincerely together, not only for the Church, but also, of course, for the future of our institution.

Summer university

Angers, summer university, 6-11 July 2009: truth and life

Two institutions with very different profiles – the Faculty of Theology of the Catholic University of the West (UCO) and Domuni – decided to join forces to organise a convivial meeting, providing an opportunity for theological reflection. The programme alternated between lectures and workshops, enabling participants to develop their own reflections on God while broadening their knowledge through interaction with specialist academics. The week offered an overview of the fundamentals of theology, including the Bible, dogma, ethics and history. For our fledgling institution, it was a chance to be welcomed by a well-established academic structure for the first time. It was a valuable educational experience for everyone

---

[97] Jérôme Carcopino, *Les Fouilles de Saint-Pierre et la tradition* (The Saint-Pierre Excavations and Tradition), Albin Michel, 1963, Paris.

involved, with beneficial courses being shared, marking a successful beginning to our collaboration.

París, summer university, 5-8 July 2010: The God of life

As it was easier to bring students and teachers together in Paris than in the provinces, the summer university was better attended there than in Angers, with high-profile speakers such as Marie Balmary and Dominique Ponau. Discreetly joining the participants at the back of the room was Brother Bruno Cadoré, who was then President of Domuni and Provincial of the Dominicans. Sometimes he would sit on the steps in front of the entrance, on the sidelines of the lecture he had given. For him, as for many other brothers, it was a great opportunity to meet students and teachers. Vatican Radio did a nice interview about the event[98].

The aim of the summer university was to meet people. As most teaching takes place remotely, it was important to make the most of the participants' physical presence to forge connections. The focus was on cultural outings in Paris, including a private visit to the Louvre, where the theology implicit in certain religious works was explored.

The photos show that the 2010 summer university was not as challenging as theology can sometimes be. Brother Pedro Meca's camaraderie and Brother Antoine Lion's expertise remain unforgettable. The Musée des Arts Forains[99] took us on a wild ride on 19th century carousels, a far cry from today's safety standards... A different way of embodying the circumincession evoked by the morning's dogmatists, but above all a way of experiencing wonder and celebration. The life-size horses were not intended for children, but for adults who, in the past, would buy themselves a ride on the merry-go-round to imagine, for a moment, that they belonged to the privileged social class that owned a horse.

---

[98] See the recording in the archives.

[99] Every year, Brother Pedro Meca and his association organised a Christmas party for the homeless.

Rhuys, summer university, 23-28 August 2011: Philosophers and theologians on the shores of faith

The workshops offered an opportunity to discover major texts, to acquire a theological culture and to practise debating. The philosopher stimulated theological discourse by providing issues and tools for thought. The theologian communicated the insights of Revelation to the philosopher. He brought the spiritual experience of the believing people, the wisdom of a tradition, a collective history and a divine promise.

We "lived the sea" with an oceanic feeling. This was not only because we were staying in a historic property on a cliff facing the ocean – a monastery that had once offered refuge to the famous Abelard in the Middle Ages – but also because a sense of team spirit, friendship and peaceful contemplation gradually formed during our intellectual and spiritual journeys.

Time was set aside for relaxation: walking along the customs path; chatting on the terraces of the medieval village; swimming on the beach; and sailing in the Gulf of Morbihan. At the 2011 summer university, which addressed big questions on the edge of faith, all those willing to ask themselves questions were invited to attend.

Speakers included the vicar general of the diocese, Father Bernard Théraud; Brother Charles Morerod, rector of the Angelicum; and teachers from Domuni: Emmanuel Boissieu; Sister Marie Monnet; Brother Michel Van Aerde; Pierre-Yves Materne; Dominique Collin; and Brother Jean-Yves Brachet. New connections stimulated the students and enabled the teachers to adapt their methods. A boat cruise under grey skies punctuated by magnificent sunny spells finally allowed us to experience the fresh air of the Gulf of Morbihan.

Rhuys, Summer University, 2012: Talking to God, talking about God

Unfortunately, due to a backlog of dates, the second event in Rhuys in 2012 took place too late in the summer. In order to balance the budget, we limited the number of speakers: Brother Dominique Charles, Father Bruno Callebaut, Brother Patrick Lens, Father Bernard Théraud, Brother Michel Van Aerde and Sister Marie

Monnet, with Sister Anne Lécu, already on site, invited by the Lay Dominicans.

The announcement of the event was beautiful: *Do not take the name of God in vain*. Current events have shown the extent to which the word "God" has been used to justify abominable crimes. How could we free ourselves from this? Could we not speak of God as if He were the friend we had met, in an indescribable face-to-face encounter that was impossible to keep to ourselves? It was at the heart of this last paradox, and because we wanted our theology to be as spiritual, pneumatic and, let us say it, theological as possible, that we set up our Summer University: *How to say the unspeakable?*

New languages and international development

Domuni's intuition, the confirmation of the General Chapters and the call of the Masters of the Order all pointed in an international direction. Although cyberspace made it technically possible to cross geographical borders, linguistic borders remained. Depending on the Order's structure, it was possible to rapidly establish a network of training centres offering instruction in a variety of languages. The Spanish were the first to be approached.

The Province of Toulouse shared borders with the Province of Spain in Europe, Peru and Haiti. However, contact was kept to a minimum. I had been following the online developments of the Escuela de Salamanca under Brother Francisco Farago and his young computer scientists. It was at the Atocha convent that I met Alan Rives, creator of the last public site and of Domoodle, our teaching platform. After much hesitation, an agreement was signed with the *Junta de los provinciales de Iberica*. Their courses were integrated into the HIRS Domuni programme.

To develop teaching in English, we contacted the Irish Dominicans at Priory Institute, then the English Dominicans at Oxford and Cambridge, we signed an agreement with the Dominican University in Ibadan, Nigeria, we went to Canada, to Toronto in particular, and then to South Africa. We discovered the very modern University of Pietermaritzburg in KwaZulu-Natal, where Brother Philippe Denis, a Belgian by birth, taught and was Regent of Studies.

New Dominican teachers joined us, who are highly competent in human rights, such as Brother Stanlaus Muyebe, or in philosophy, such as Brother Isaac Mutelo. An English-language magazine was created. The collaboration was genuine and they chose my proposal for the name of their journal: JOCAP, Journal of Contemporary African Philosophy.

As English is the *lingua franca*, teachers came from all over the world, from the USA and the United Kingdom, of course, but also from Australia, Croatia, Austria, Israel, Italy, Germany, Canada, India, South Africa, and so on.

Ask and ye shall receive. We appealed to the Indian Dominicans. Some of them had come to Belgium to do their doctorate in Leuven. They were very accommodating and provided excellent teaching in subjects such as Bible, theology, philosophy, human rights and Indian philosophy. The Indian subcontinent's contribution was an opportunity, given its unfathomable cultural wealth and the dynamism of this young province.

Arabic is a language that is very different from European languages. It is written from right to left and uses a special alphabet. This poses no technical problem; we could just as easily teach in Chinese, Vietnamese, Bengali or Tamil – Moodle is pre-programmed for that. The difficulty lies more in internal communication to ensure that the quality is the same in all the languages.

Brother Ameer Jajé is the linchpin of the Arabic programmes. Warm and always encouraging, well-versed in academic matters with his doctorate from the University of Strasbourg, he has many resources at his disposal thanks to his international network of teaching friends. Firmly rooted in Iraq, but always on the move with his French passport, between Egypt, Rome, Turkey, Lebanon, Jordan and Europe, Ameer has gradually completed the courses required for a bachelor's degree, then various master's degrees in theology, not forgetting university certificates. Elise Saad, a Lebanese trilingual translator who works from Beirut, has patiently harmonised best practices.

A full range of courses in Arabic, including bachelor's, master's and PhD courses in theology, are available online. It is run by a network of teachers. Publications of books in Arabic have begun.

Engaging in inter-religious dialogue allows us to organise conferences with universities that are far removed from us, both ideologically and geographically. For example, I am thinking of the mullahs from Kufa who came to Paris. Had it not been for the Iran-Israel war, we would have met them at their place for the "return match" of a conference on the role of women in Christianity and Islam.

The "Domuni instrument" offers unique and exceptional potential here, too. Research takes place at the heart of practice, in action and commitment, as recommended by *Veritatis Gaudium*.

Civil recognition

The desire for recognition is an unquenchable thirst, a fire that consumes many human beings. René Girard analyses it in *Mensonge romantique et vérité romanesque* (Romantic Lies and Romantic Truths) by identifying the "obstacle model", the character whose good graces, encouragement and above all recognition a person seeks, like a drug that never delivers the desired level of satisfaction.

René Girard would be 100 years old today. I was delighted to read his works, to write an introductory course, to offer several seminars on his thought, and finally to meet him! He sheds light on the difficulty of recognition. The trap of mimetic desire is a formidable one, and I think I was able to avoid it, both for myself and for our association. The question kept coming back: *Are you recognised?* In the early years, I answered with a smile. *By whom are Oxford or Cambridge recognised? By whom was Socrates recognised? By whom is the Pope recognised? By whom is God recognised?* When the person I was talking to was able to understand it, I would comment on the question put to Jesus: *By what authority are you doing this?*[100] The question is theological and metaphysical, not just social or psychological.

---

[100] Mt 21:23: *[...] the chief priests and the elders of the people came unto Him as He was teaching and said, "By what authority doest thou these things? And who gave thee this authority?" And Jesus answered and said unto them, "I also will ask you one thing, which if ye tell Me, I in like manner will tell you by what authority I do these things. The baptism of John: whence was it? From Heaven, or of men?" And they reasoned among*

In front of the burning bush, Moses asked his interlocutor *What is your name?* He answers *I Am That I Am*, a complicated expression in Hebrew because it is in the unaccomplished tense, a tense that should be translated instead as *I will be who I will be* or *I will be with you who you will see* – or, more colloquially, *You will see what I am made of*, since the bush is not consumed. Every person is a mystery, a mystery to others and a mystery to ourselves. And sometimes, we have to affirm ourselves. Here, God is self-affirming: *I am*. The Christian God is more than that; He is also relationship. Theologians make this clear: in the Trinity, relationship is constitutive of the person.

So, as Brother Claude Geffré writes, *God is absolutely relative*, and this has nothing to do with any kind of relativism. To say *absolutely relative* is not a contradiction, it is a perfect model of relationship and reciprocity. If this is so for God, how is it for us? Who recognises me? Who makes me exist? Who addresses me to summon me? These are themes that Domuni teaches through many thinkers, from Aristotle to Michel Henry, not forgetting Pascal, Descartes and Levinas.

So, is it any wonder that, as an institution, Domuni is faced with this existential question? What we teach, we also experience, sometimes painfully, often happily.

The University of Lorraine, 25 April 2013

Some issues move forward naturally, while others remain blocked, no matter how hard we try. With the University of Lorraine, thanks to the intelligence and diplomacy of Brother Jacques Fantino, who was the director of the Centre Autonome d'Enseignement et de Pédagogie Religieuse (CAEPR, Autonomous Centre for Religious Teaching and Pedagogy) at the University of Lorraine, I was able to sign an agreement with the president of the university that has been renewed ever since. The agreement enables us to offer students French national bachelor's and master's degrees in theology. Only the universities of Lorraine and Strasbourg offer these diplomas

---

themselves, saying, "If we shall say, 'From heaven,' he will say unto us, 'Why did ye not then believe him?' But if we shall say, 'Of men,' we fear the people, for all hold John to be a prophet." And they answered Jesus and said, "We cannot tell." And He said unto them, "Neither tell I you by what authority I do these things."

because, to put it briefly, they are concordat departments: they were German at the time of the separation of Church and State. They benefited from special conditions at the time of reunification in 1918.

This agreement, drawn up by the legal services of the state university, was signed by *Pierre Muntzenhardt, President of the University of Lorraine, and Michel Van Aerde, Director General of Domuni University*. It should be noted that no French government body[101] has ever criticised Domuni for using the word "university". It is the Congregation for Catholic Education and a few ecclesiastics who, out of a lack of self-esteem, point out that in France this term is reserved for public higher education establishments.

The theology department at the University of Lorraine experienced some challenging years when the local bishop, under pressure from the Congregation for Catholic Education – anxious to isolate future priests from public university courses – stopped sending his seminarians there. He claimed that they were not receiving teaching adapted to their needs, such as a more detailed course on the Eucharist. The director of the CAEPR and I met with the bishop and shared several meals with him, but we were unable to convince him of our point of view.

Following the diocesan seminary's distancing itself from the theology department, there was a drop in enrolments which could have led to the department's closure (in the end, it was the seminary that was closed). However, our school's enrolments made up for this loss. On several occasions, the professors from Lorraine expressed their gratitude for being "saved", until the introduction of the national "Parcoursup" programme put them out of harm's way. Thanks to their distance learning programme, they were able to recruit students from all over France.

Many Master's dissertations are supervised by Metz lecturers. They sit on examination panels and contribute their expertise. Anecdotally, a Master's dissertation in Church History that was graded 20/20 caused quite a stir. *20/20 is supposed to be an unattainable grade!* Professor Sylvie Barnay, from the University of Lorraine and director of the dissertation, stood firm. It transpired that

---

[101] Nor do the Belgians at UCLouvain.

the student was a doctor with an Habilitation to Direct Research (HDR) who was teaching on the island of La Réunion. This was no exception. Another university lecturer had followed his entire career, but had requested confidentiality. Or we were surprised to discover, after the fact, that the rector of one of France's largest Catholic institutes had stealthily completed a master's degree in philosophy at Domuni. With the highest honours, no less!

Jerusalem (EBAF), 2015

Since 2015, an agreement has been in place with Brother Olivier-Thomas Venard, director of the *La Bible En Ses Traditions* (BEST, The Bible In Its Traditions) research programme at the École Biblique et Archéologique Française de Jérusalem (EBAF), to offer a joint master's degree on the reception of the Bible. The students' final work is published by Domuni-Press.

This proximity led BEST to set itself up as a Belgian International Non-Profit Association (AISBL), domiciled at Aqua Viva, Brussels, and managed by Sister Marie Monnet, like the Belgian association Domuni Europe. It subsequently set itself up as a publishing house. In return, our school organised a study session for around thirty students in Jerusalem, on the premises of the École Biblique and with its researchers.

Belgium and UCLouvain

I lived in Belgium for seventeen years, from 2005 to 2022. Given my love of sunshine and dislike of damp climates, that is a long time. How do you explain my choice of Brussels after my time in the provinces and the end of my convalescence? The dilemma was this: should I go back to Latin America? Or should I return to Montpellier, which I left in 1992?

My criterion was apostolic. If Peter and Paul had gone to Rome, could I choose Washington or Beijing? European integration was underway, which interested me. There was an international Dominican community there, and its church was the closest to the Berlaymont building, home to the European Commission.

Five kilometres away, Marie Monnet was part of the community of *Saint Mary Magdalene, Apostle of the Apostles*. This was a group of sisters who preached and lived the Dominican life as the friars did. I was also interested in this initiative of feminine preaching.

Living in Brussels, a stone's throw from the European Union and the *European Village*, immersed me in a young, social and cosmopolitan bubble. It was an opportunity to revisit the history of the world wars and reconciliation in places where the memory of Jean Monnet, Alcide de Gasperi, Paul Henri Spaak and Robert Schuman was still very much alive. *L'Europe difficile* (The Difficult Europe)[102] was one of my first reads. Was our little project any easier?

The intonations of conversations in the bars made my ears sensitive to an incredible variety of languages. I soon met several European civil servants, including Yves Moiny, a high-level official whose eldest son I christened. He was a Belgian magistrate who worked in fraud control, particularly in relation to Romania. His legal advice to the association was invaluable. Robert Madelin, a stylish British former Oxford and ENA graduate and a devout Catholic, was married to an atheist Frenchwoman and was the CEO of an EU Directorate-General. From the outset, he saw the Domuni venture as very promising, as he did the Espaces venture, which I was managing at the time. He welcomed the young European Dominicans we had invited to discover the European institutions to his offices, where simultaneous translation was provided. He made a remark that did not fall on deaf ears: to animate a dispersed network, a critical mass of talent in one place was necessary.

Bearing this in mind, we decided to bring our key collaborators together in an international office at the Dominican Sisters of Acqua Viva's home. Rather than renting out a few student rooms, Marie Monnet transformed the premises to provide Domuni with a functional area comprising bright, spacious offices, a kitchen and a reception room. The office was located 100 metres from the underground station and was set in the middle of a welcoming

---

[102] Alessandro Giacone and Bino Olivi. *L'Europe difficile : Histoire politique de la construction européenne* (The Difficult Europe: A Political History of the Construction of Europe). 2007. Poche

garden. It was wonderful on sunny days. I arrived in the late morning or early afternoon and did not leave until nightfall. The team was international: There were English, Belgian, French and Italian people, as well as Lebanese people, and trainees from Cameroon, Greece and Japan. Was it more effective than the current remote working team? The energy required to run it was enormous, but I have not regretted the change.

I had to make an effort to adapt to life in Belgium. This was in line with our institution's efforts to become more international. In order to experience the richness that transculturality brought, you had to accept the discomfort of constantly switching from one language to another. Our vocabulary was smaller: we used words like "wipe", "rag" and "support" to describe objects that the French had more precise terms for. Under the influence of Dutch, we spoke of a "brol" or a "kot", and it was "difficult" to express ourselves differently. Otherness was always present. This stimulated openness, but it could also be exhausting. While only 6 languages were spoken at the UN, 27 were spoken at the European Union! Was our institution to become Belgian? Would Brussels become the capital of Europe? It was a close call. Teleworking turned this dynamic on its head in an unforeseeable way.

I quickly realised the potential for collaboration between UCLouvain and Domuni. Given where our institution was in 2005, the idea would have been laughable, yet this dream slowly became a reality[103]. Professor Arnaud Join-Lambert, Professor of Practical Theology, was the first to visit us at Acqua Viva. After his election as vice-dean of the Faculty of Theology, Professor Régis Burnet followed suit, and a formal meeting with the teaching staff was finally organised on the faculty premises in Louvain-La-Neuve, opposite the central square.

The Master in Biblical Studies (EBIB) is a joint degree. It carries the logo of each of the universities. Students are selected on the basis of their level of proficiency in the biblical languages – Hebrew, Greek and Aramaic. This master's degree focuses heavily on historical-critical exegesis, appealing only to a small number of

---

[103] This had not been possible with the Catholic University of Toulouse.

students. Paradoxically, it is the Domuni teachers who must bear the brunt of UCLouvain's decision to prioritise ancient languages. As teachers of biblical languages are becoming increasingly scarce, recruitment internationally is a viable option, whereas this is very difficult locally. On 8 June 2023, collaboration opened up to include a joint Bachelor of Theology degree, which will attract many more students. As our institution is no longer centred in Belgium, no one thinks in terms of rivalry. The distance clears the air.

Master's and bachelor's degrees take place on the Domuni platform and are regulated by its administration. Lecturers upload their lessons to Do-Moodle and can update them as they wish.

Brother Augustin Wiliwoli

Ori Originally from Isiro in the DRC, Brother Augustin is a wise man, and above all a cautious one. The first time we met, he sat back in his armchair, listened, and spoke little. He was discovering Europe. Three years after his arrival, he has adapted perfectly. Having financed his own education through numerous pastoral activities, he successfully completed his doctorate in philosophy at UCLouvain. The defence was clear and convincing.

The subject was both academic and highly topical, in his own country as in many other places: *De la lutte pour l'existence à la lutte pour la reconnaissance* (From the Struggle for Existence to the Struggle for Recognition). As a teacher at Domuni, he was Director of the Africa Department (DAF) and then Dean of the Faculty of Philosophy. The DAF cuts across disciplines, and we have to take into account the cultural and economic specificities of students' countries of origin. Together with his compatriot Apollinaire Kivyamunda and a growing number of other colleagues, Brother Augustin Wiliwoli enables our institution to be African as well as European. Dean of the Faculty of Philosophy, living in Kinshasa, Brother Augustin wisely kept his post when he was elected provincial of the Dominicans of the DRC and, with a seriousness that gives him a natural authority, he remains available and faithful to his commitments.

Various agreements have been signed with African university centres: the University of Uélé (DRC), the University of the

Assumption in Congo (UAC), the ICJM in Mauritius, the Cathedral School of Bafoussan in Cameroon, the Dominican University of Ibadan (Nigeria), the Dominicans of South Africa, the Université Catholique de Madagascar (UCM), the University of Tangaza (Kenya), the Saint Dominic University of West Africa (USDAO), the Dominican Institute of Oriental Studies (IDEO, Cairo, Egypt)...

> **Why are theological training centres closing?**
>
> The Institute of Theological Studies (IÉT), founded by the Jesuits in Brussels in 1968, closed in 2019, 50 years after its creation. Its closure was announced on its website in 2017[104]. The reasons were financial: *The effort made in terms of people and finances has proved increasingly difficult to sustain over the years.* What were the IÉT's objectives? The satisfaction of the message states it unambiguously: *The Faculty has trained more than 1,100 priests. Seven of them are now bishops. The Society of Jesus is happy to have been able to contribute to their formation and expresses its great gratitude to all the bishops and leaders who have placed their trust in us, as well as to the many non-Jesuit professors who have contributed to this important service to the Church.* When we speak of the "Church", it is mainly from a clerical point of view. What seems to count is the number of priests and bishops. I am sure that this implicit ecclesiology is at odds with the one that was taught.
>
> On the advice of an American Dominican who taught at the IÉT and was staying in my convent, one kilometre away, I wrote to the superior asking him if we could not think together about the possibility of collaborating to continue offering degree courses. I received no reply. Today I read on the website: *After numerous exchanges and discussions with the Institute's main partners, in dialogue with the Archbishopric of Malines-Brussels, the Superior General of the Society of Jesus has taken the decision to ask the Congregation for Catholic Education to suspend the Faculty in September 2019.* Everything had been decided in advance and in high places. The main reason for the closure was the decline in the number of future priests in training and the repatriation to France of the training of French seminarians.
>
> In 2010, the bishops of French-speaking Belgium (Namur, Liège, Tournai, Malines-Bruxelles) pooled their resources for theological training at the major seminary in Namur[105]. Why have they not joined forces with the faculty of

---

[104] "L'Institut d'Études Théologiques à Bruxelles repense son avenir" (The Institute of Theological Studies in Brussels rethinks its future), on the Jesuits website, Brussels, 28 June 2017. [Online].

[105] See: www.seminairedenamur.be/histoire-du-seminaire.

theology at UCLouvain, where the dioceses do not have to pay for the teaching staff?

Lumen Vitae, International Catechetical and Pastoral Institute, set the scene on its portal: *Private establishment: training and academic qualifications are not recognised by the French Community of Belgium*, although courses are valued in European credits (ECTS).

Initially based in Brussels, it moved to Namur in 2016. *Our aim is to train religious men and women, priests and laypeople, whatever their initial level of theological training.*

I used to teach at the Lumen Vitae Centre from time to time, so the link with Domuni was a natural one until we signed an agreement on 23 December 2006. Lumen Vitae has copied the way our school works, in part, by creating its own teaching platform for uploading videos. However, it was blended learning that blocked the remote enrolment of students, as some of the courses were face-to-face. Due to a lack of staff, the Brussels site was closed.

The days of training in Europe for Africans, South Americans and Asians were over, as training was increasingly provided in their countries of origin. This was not a cause for regret: the students who had trained in Europe had obtained doctorates and then organised training in their countries of origin. Was this not precisely what we could have hoped for?

The Dominican College of Ottawa, founded in 1900, also closed its doors on 31 December 2023. It affiliated with Carleton University in 2012 and successfully completed the *Institutional Quality Assurance Process (IQAP) in 2013 and 2017.*

The undergraduate and postgraduate programmes in philosophy and theology were fully accredited and funded by the Department for Higher Education and Skills[106]. What more could you ask for? And yet these qualities were not enough.

Here and there across Europe, theology faculties stand empty, devoid of both students and teachers. Dead branches are breaking off amid general indifference. Where is the Spirit of the Risen One blowing? At one of the first General Assemblies of our association, Brother Bruno Cadoré shared a memory. In 1968, when many ecclesiastical institutions were collapsing, the Provincial of France made the following comment: *When the apostles were meeting and discussing the procedure for replacing Judas, Saint Paul was already in action.* The Spirit blows where it wills. He does not always make it known and rarely respects the hierarchy, which almost always leads to discomfort in terms of recognition.

---

[106] See: https://udominicaine.ca/historique.

The French Higher Education Department

The first form of recognition was as an association under the 1901 law – a not-for-profit legal entity. It was subsequently recognised as a private higher education establishment by the Higher Education Department of the Rectorate of the Academy of Toulouse (DESUP). I can recall a few memories of this stage.

It all started with a visit to the Rectorate of the Academy of Toulouse, to the Director of Higher Education, Ms Y. and her assistant, Mr M. It was still possible to meet them in their offices. Several forms were completed and the required documents were presented.

We wrote to the relevant people regarding their criminal records and received the documents directly, certifying that they were clean. Regarding the building's compliance with safety standards and the fire brigade's certificate, Ms Y. explained that these were not applicable. On 23 March 2011, less than two months after submitting our application, we received confirmation that our "course" had been authorised and registered. Mr M. showed us our application, which was similar to that of the Catholic University of Toulouse. Every time we visited, we received a warm welcome:

> *These are the friends from Domuni, exclaimed Mrs Y. I hope retirement comes soon so I can enrol!*

However, with the advent of jihadist terrorism, everything changed. We no longer had access to the offices, which had moved to the newly built Rectorate building in the meantime. Most importantly, Mr M. had been replaced by someone completely different: barefoot, wearing flip-flops, and dressed in a way that matched his appearance. He erected a tall wall between the DESUP and us, not responding to requests for appointments and refusing to see us for more than a few minutes in the entrance hall. When I pointed out to him that the philosophy faculty at the University of Toulouse had not responded to a request for an agreement, he replied, *Well, of course!* Was lack of courtesy the rule in French universities? We had presented him with a request for a *Rectoral Jury* for philosophy, and he had never replied, despite our repeated requests. A combination of pure chance then occurred, with a series of improbable events that I would like to dwell on, because we could read in them the mysterious influence of an invisible presence. Are we being supported?

I will have to backtrack a little here. On 1 September 2008, Domuni and the Theology Faculty of the Catholic University of the West (UCO) signed a collaboration agreement. Under this agreement, our institution offered UCO a reserved space on its Moodle platform for distance learning courses. A handful of teachers took advantage of this opportunity, including a philosopher from UCO, who offered two courses. Several years later, he sent me an email asking for his CV to be removed from the list of teachers, and finally for his courses to be removed from any web page on our institution's sites. This was done without delay. In an anti-clerical context, he explained, he could not risk being identified with our institution when he was taking national competitive examinations. We complied without difficulty. He passed the exam and was eventually appointed inspector for philosophy in the Toulouse academy: ours, by chance. And what a chance!

We had never met, having only exchanged e-mails. Taking advantage of a trip to Toulouse, we phoned him. He was due to catch a train within the hour. As we were driving close to the Rectorate, we gave him a lift. Between the Rectorate and Gare Saint-Agne, we told him about our problem with the Rectoral Jury and he took it upon himself to investigate.

That is how we found out that our application had been put on hold because there was no inspector of philosophy in the academy: the position had not yet been filled... Until our new friend assumed the position. The application had therefore been presented to an arts inspector (!) who had given a negative opinion, as the courses were not, in his opinion, of a good standard.

How could this unknown inspector assess courses to which he had no access? Our friend got the Higher Education Department to take charge of our case. We opened up the philosophy courses on the teaching platform to him by sending him the necessary codes and he read all the courses. His assessment focused on the following areas: the title; the quality of each course; how the three years were organised; the teachers' CVs and diplomas (master's degrees, doctorates, École Normale Supérieure qualifications, Agrégation qualifications); foreign language courses; and assessment methods. While the full report rejected some courses, it did not mention any of them by name. Certain courses or parts of courses were rejected on the grounds of secularism (for example, the philosophical question of the existence of God). It also asked for a few additional courses. These adjustments were made and the new assessment was entirely positive. Our application was complete, all that was missing was the decision of the Rector of the Toulouse academy.

We never received this decision, which shows that the school war is still not over, that anti-clericalism is raging and that the ministries are acting in bad faith. Rather than rejecting us outright, they chose not to respond. Should we have looked outside France?

A Belgian friend organised an evening at his home in Brussels with the director of the FNRS, the Belgian equivalent of the French CNRS. The latter's husband, an entrepreneur, was fond of our company's model. His wife, on the other hand, was somewhat surprised, and began by asking our mutual friend how he could associate with Catholic clerics. It seemed that she was hinting at their shared membership of the Freemasons. While describing Belgian universities as deeply divided and riven with rivalry between rectors, she explained that it was impossible for another university, especially a denominational one, to emerge on the academic landscape of the kingdom[107].

Where to settle? Even more than Belgium, Switzerland had the advantage of being multilingual – with German, French and Italian – and open to the international community. Geneva was home to numerous UN offices and agencies, including the UNHCR, IOM and ILO. Switzerland was therefore the obvious choice.

Switzerland

We therefore set up the Domuni-Suisse association, with its headquarters in the convent in Geneva. This was in a very desirable location, not far from the French border and just a few minutes from Lake Geneva. This small convent had a few rooms, a large and

---

[107] Those in the know will recognise the allusion to the "landscape law".

beautiful church and a library. Brother Michel Fontaine was the prior; he taught at Domuni and was in favour of the project. The Dominican provincial of Switzerland, Br Guido Vergauwen, former rector of the University of Fribourg and former assistant for the intellectual life of the Master of the Order, had solid international university experience. He was able to help our association in its dealings with the Swiss ministry. The association brought together a number of students, former students and teachers who had taken part in the sessions in Jerusalem and Jordan, and were all highly respected professionals.

Yves Guisan was a surgeon, Swiss consul in Gibraltar and former member of parliament; Guy was an architect; Pascal Bregnard was head of the Catholic Centre in Lausanne and later became director of Caritas for the Diocese of Fribourg; Jean-Louis Meylan had a doctorate in education and worked in Lausanne; Barbara von Orelli was a senior lecturer and professor of art history at the University of Zurich. Marie-Antoinette Lorwich, a former banker who had converted to Christianity, was employed by the diocese to care for the homeless in Lausanne. Nicole Awaïs had a doctorate in theology and taught at Domuni, as well as working at the United Nations High Commission for Refugees in Geneva. Many theology professors at Fribourg University had taught one or more courses at Domuni, including Luc Devillers, Gilles Emery, Benoît-Dominique de La Soujeole, Jean-Louis Poffet, Michel Fontaine and Philippe Lefebvre, among others.

The director of the Agency of Accreditation and Quality Assurance (AAQ), accompanied by his assistant, was invited by Brother Guido Vergauwen to meet us in his office at the University of Fribourg. He showed great interest in the project and guaranteed a 99% chance of success. An initial project was to be drawn up and presented by the AAQ to the Federal Accreditation Council. The AAQ would assist us in drafting the application. Following a one-day pre-visit, and then a three-day visit, an expert report would be drawn up by the AAQ and submitted to the Federal Council for approval.

We were delighted. In Switzerland, you had to pay to take these steps, and afterwards it was clear and professional. The archives show the many exchanges that took place with the AAQ in a process that lasted several years. The process involved drafting the articles of association for the Swiss association, the Academic Senate, the faculty councils, a presentation of the general pedagogical approach, the courses on offer, the courses with all the necessary details, vision, mission, quality system and so on. The very heavy application was printed and distributed at the time of the "visit" to each of the AAQ experts. The experts' pre-visit took place at the convent in Geneva. The visit, on the other hand, took place on the premises of the University of Fribourg.

We quickly noticed a change in attitude on the part of the AAQ. The secretary, B. F., had stayed on, while the person leading the discussions had been changed. While the former was open and positive, the latter, L. B., was quite the opposite. She had raised objections from the outset and her approach was not really the smartest one. *Why do you want to develop a distance learning university when all universities already teach by distance learning – there is nothing original about that!* And so on. Rather than helping us write the application, she spent her time looking for flaws and asking for additional documents. The meeting minutes she wrote were so biased that we had to change several paragraphs each time. Towards the end of the process, she explicitly advised us to postpone the "visit" and presentation of our application. She officially argued that we were not ready, but her real reasons were that we were presenting a model that she did not accept (100% distance learning) and that we were not Swiss enough – too Belgian and French. The bad faith was obvious, and our Swiss friends called it *Swissness*.

I wanted us to push the process as far as possible because I thought it would be useful to decipher the demands and mysteries of an academic world that uses the words "science", "research" and "autonomy" at every turn to conceal its unavowable interests. We were not alone: all Swiss universities were undergoing the same process of institutional accreditation. Some were approved straight away, like the University of Lausanne, while others were refused or delayed. One might well wonder whether the newcomers were subjected to some kind of "hazing", not to mention the accreditation agencies' financial interests.

Officially, the entire application was based on quality criteria. It had to be demonstrated that the implemented quality system could ensure systematic operation leading to almost automatic progression. Anglo-Saxon culture reigned supreme, and as good students, we had learnt the vocabulary and grammar.

According to a friend who is the director of the largest hospital in Brussels, the quality system we presented surpassed anything he had ever seen. However, our AAQ contact was not deterred. As far as she was concerned, it looked good on paper, but it had not yet worked well enough. *The AAQ is not assessing a project,* she explained, *it is assessing how it works on a regular basis.* In reality, the decision had been made even before the assessment took place. Proof of this was that no expert had spent more than 15 minutes looking at the courses on the Moodle platform, and some had not logged on at all. We had kept screenshots of the activity reports provided by the teaching platform and could prove who had opened which page and for how long.

In addition, the way the AAQ operated in no way corresponded to the humanist principles demanded of its clients: the experts showed an undisguised reluctance to talk to the African teachers, calling them by their first name instead of their surname, and not addressing them with proper etiquette. Furthermore, with the way the AAQ operated, there was no possibility of appeal.

In this process of recognition, we were faced with the eternal question of the chicken and the egg: how can we exist if we are not recognised, and how can we be recognised if we have not yet begun to exist? Fortunately, we did exist and had received various recognitions that the AAQ had not wanted to consider, including those from the Order of Preachers, the Holy See (as an HIRS), the French State (as a private higher education establishment) and the universities that had signed collaboration agreements.

Y. G., a former Swiss federal deputy and member of the association, shared his thoughts with me:

> *I fully agree with your thoughts on "recognition". They clearly go beyond the usual formalism that I am fighting against with you. However, there are some inescapable contingencies: the skills and knowledge acquired must receive official recognition (a diploma) if they are to be put to good use subsequently in any activity plan whatsoever. This*

is what Domuni does with its French, Belgian and Catholic Education recognition.

The mutual recognition of degrees instituted by the EU (of which Bologna is an instrument) means that degrees awarded by Domuni are also valid in Switzerland, with or without official registration by the university. A new attempt is therefore of no practical significance whatsoever. The AAQ process was a total disgrace, a feeling that already pervaded me in the corridors of the University of Fribourg.

On the other hand, your quality option is likely to humble the proud punisher by taking them down a peg. This is indeed the way forward, and I fully agree with you on this point. Quality solves all problems, whether they involve Swiss sensitivities or marketing.[108]

The institutional accreditation we were seeking in Switzerland, we already had in France, as a "private higher education establishment" with an UAI number, recognised by the Ministry of Education and Research, and "general interest" status recognised by the Ministry of the Economy and Finance. Our French status allowed us to exist and, like some French universities, such as the University of Toulouse for economics, to teach in other languages.

In our search for recognition, we experienced a lack of self-awareness or self-confidence, a lack of awareness of our own worth. So, to answer the question of *who recognises you*, all we had to do was refer to the thirty or so universities that had signed a collaboration agreement with Domuni Universitas. In the French-speaking world, our collaboration with the University of Louvain-la-Neuve, the University of Lorraine and the ICES in La Roche-sur-Yon carried a lot of weight. Our institution was a member of the UNFL and the European Union of Private Higher Education (EUPHE). So, the issue was already addressed at the institutional level. However, this experience encouraged us to explore its philosophical and theological ramifications[109].

---

[108] Private email of 4/01/2020.

[109] See Paul Ricœur's final work, *Parcours de la reconnaissance* (Journey to Recognition). Axel Honneth, *La Lutte pour la reconnaissance* (The Struggle for Recognition). See the

When we ask the question of recognition, we need to be clear: from whom? Should we seek recognition from the authorities (ministries, etc.)? Should we seek recognition from our competitors? We have already answered that question, insofar as competitors can become partners by signing collaboration agreements. Should we seek recognition from teachers? Without them, we would not be able to offer any teaching. Should we seek recognition from students? This is measured in terms of membership and growth in registrations. It is expressed in the reviews posted on Google, in the "expressions of recognition" in the sense of thanks. Ultimately, should recognition from employers not be considered the most important? Mr Blondel, Rector of UCLouvain, insisted on this during a meeting prior to the signing of our collaboration agreement.

The quality of a university is undoubtedly measured by the way it responds to the concrete needs of society. Domuni students have no problem finding employment as diocesan animators in Switzerland, Belgium, France and Cameroon, as chaplains (Saint-Luc hospital in Brussels, French army) or teachers (Côte d'Ivoire, South Africa), and those who have studied philosophy or other disciplines can testify that these complementary courses are much appreciated by their employers and that they have been promoted.

In response to a pressing and repeated request to define ourselves, we run the risk of comparing ourselves with other institutions. They are similar in that they pursue the same objectives: teaching and research. They are different in the way they achieve them. They are localised, Domuni is not. They have opted for blended learning, while we teach entirely by distance learning. Our school has a flexible relationship with space and time. If we add transdisciplinarity, transculturality and the management of an international network, we can see that our university is certainly a compatible mutation, but irreducible to the entities with which some would like to compare it.

---

thesis by Augustin Wiliwoli, Dean of the Faculty of Philosophy at Domuni: *De la lutte pour l'existence à la lutte pour la reconnaissance* (From the Struggle for Existence to the Struggle for Recognition).

Some international events

To facilitate communication, meetings lasting a few days are highly beneficial, helping to build team spirit and cohesion. The Journées d'Études Participatives (JEP, Participatory Study Days), where students and teachers exchange ideas on a cross-disciplinary theme, are very easy to organise. Summer universities are more complex, and far-flung conferences even more complicated, especially in high-risk countries such as Kurdistan or Iraq, Lebanon or Colombia. Ad hoc meetings are needed to meet the IT people in Madrid, or to visit the offices in Rome.

Let us take a look at a few face-to-face events.

Spain: Salamanca, July 2014

The international colloquium *On the Sources of Liberalism and Fundamental Rights* brought together around twenty researchers in law, theology, philosophy, history and social sciences at the San Esteban Faculty of Theology in Salamanca, on the very site where, four centuries earlier, Francisco de Vitoria and his first disciples lived. The Order of Preachers was celebrating its 800th anniversary. As Marie Monnet wrote in her introduction to the Colloquium Proceedings, published on Domuni-Press:

> *In the Order of Preachers, despite all the imperfections of human nature, we are deeply convinced that law is the incarnation of love and that true love requires law. As Augustin Wiliwoli emphasised in his final speech, recognising rights enables us to value others and ourselves. Vitoria and Las Casas are valuable sources for our research. They were undoubtedly accused of a little idealism! For my part, I will remember one thing: today's utopias are tomorrow's reality.*

Indonesia: Surabaya, August 2014

On the island of Java, we are meeting up with many of Domuni's teachers, in different languages, and contacting new partners. Let us read again this testimonial from Marie Monnet:

"I am taking part in the international conference *Dialogue, as a way of Preaching*, devoted to dialogue between cultures and religions, organised by Justice, Peace & Care of Creation (O.P.,

Asia/Pacific): over a hundred delegates, from the four corners of the world, with a strong Asian presence. For nearly five days, symposia, conferences, workshops and visits provided an opportunity to explore in greater depth what is a real challenge in the world of religions: dialogue. Specialists in the field – men and women who promote peace and justice – pooled their intelligence, experience and desire to mobilise, making this gathering a real success in terms of humanity, fraternity and spirituality. Those present included Brother Michel Van Aerde, Sister Marie Monnet and Brother Gustave Ineza from Rwanda, who is the coordinator of the Africa Department.

The location is symbolic. Indonesia has risen five places in six years and is now the world's tenth largest economy. This Pacific archipelago, with a population of over 252 million and located off the coast of Singapore, has considerable development potential. Indonesia is a deeply religious country, requiring every citizen to belong to a particular faith. Islam is the dominant religion, and Indonesia is the world's largest Muslim nation with around 200 million Muslims. However, Buddhism, Hinduism (particularly in Bali) and Christianity are also present in significant numbers. Indonesia is thus emblematic of the religious plurality of our globalised world.

The country is a laboratory for dialogue and a place of powerful experiences, as well as being the site of the main political issue. However, religious pluralism is based on a precarious and ever-threatened balance. Most participants are deeply committed to inter-religious dialogue and live and work in areas of high tension: Sri Lanka, Pakistan, Nigeria, Iraq, Indonesia, the Philippines, Egypt and Lebanon. There, this dialogue is not theoretical. Some of those speaking these days risk their lives daily.

Their experience of inter-religious dialogue is often one of religious intolerance, persecution and fundamentalism. The presence of these delegates cancels out any temptation to be idealistic. As one of them put it: *Despite the risks we are all too familiar with, such as kidnapping, rape and extermination, we have chosen to stay where we are in an area of intense conflict...* The thinking that develops in Surabaya emerges from these "places of incarnation"; it takes shape through experience within a context. This is the first source of richness for our conference.

The aim is therefore pragmatic: how can we promote the peaceful coexistence of cultures and religions in today's world to reduce violence and conflict? What is dialogue as a form of preaching? *We share a common goal, which is not something we have to do or be. It is something we would like to embody. Our shared belief is that we want to live together*, says Bruno Cadoré. He goes on to say that *real dialogue with others requires an internal conversation. Engaging with another culture requires us to engage with our own first. If we do not, we will have nothing to contribute to the conversation; if we cannot listen, we will not be heard.*

In Indonesia, religion is a political issue. This country, which gained independence in 1945, has a post-colonial context marked by religious pluralism, making all citizens supportive and responsible, whatever their faith. This challenges believers to integrate their faith into social life. Religious leaders have set up organisations to fight for social justice. They ensure that religious organisations do not exploit the fight against poverty to promote religious radicalism. In Yogyakarta, for instance, a consortium comprising three universities (the state university, a Muslim university, and a Christian university) is responsible for social work.

So what place is there for religion and theology in such a religious country? If Saint Paul had come to Asia, not Asia Minor, what would have been his thinking, his theology, his discourse on God? What might ours be?

The dialogue between religions is a contextualised theological space. An Indonesian speaker explains: *We are challenged to discover the presence of God in this experience of religious pluralism – that is to say, in our midst. Can we find the face of Christ in those who do not share our belief in God? Charles de Foucauld and Louis Massignon experienced the work of the Spirit at the heart of their encounters with Muslims, which transformed their lives. Their faith was revitalised through contact with a tradition that was not their own.*

What is the place of religious minorities, such as Catholics? There are very few Catholics in Asia, and Christianity is viewed as foreign. Dialogue is essential to the life of the Church in Asia. Getting to know others begins with entering into their reality. This desire for knowledge is the prerequisite for dialogue, which must be reciprocal – a challenge in itself. The desire to know others comes up against difficult, if not impossible, dialogue. It is also confronted with divisions and conflicts within the tradition of the other.

Despite the difficulties, the Dominican tradition is based on knowledge and study. According to Bruno Cadoré, *study helps to avoid the temptation to fill gaps with prejudice*: it is one of the pillars of Dominican life. The "Dominican methodology", which still needs to be perfected, provides a framework for debate. Discussions take place in an organised manner. Communion is built by calling on everyone to speak up and to dare to speak: each person has a vocation to become in turn an "actor in the conversation".

This is reminiscent of Pope Francis's words in his first official text, in which he invited everyone to engage in conversation with their neighbours and loved ones in their everyday lives. Preaching is a conversation. *Convinced that this conversation is under threat today and that many places suffer from a lack of dialogue between nations, groups of people and individuals, Dominicans are called to serve this conversation for the benefit of humanity. They can and must improve the quality of this conversation.*

What is happening in Indonesia, particularly with regard to Islam, is food for thought. We think we know others, but we do not really know them. They do not know us either. During our conference, many interesting experiences were presented that encourage mutual understanding and encounters. In particular, I would like to mention the women's groups in Indonesia who voluntarily share details of their daily lives as women and mothers. Regardless of their religious affiliation, they are able to live together and get to know each other.

Sharing life together is important, but not enough, explains a delegate living in Cairo. It is a first step in reducing fear, but we need to go further. *You have to understand the spiritual heart of other believers or non-believers*, says another delegate. Beyond the superficial aspects, *enter into the liturgy and faith of other believers*. In a context of extreme violence, this desire to know is a form of empathy that is within everyone's reach. This desire must be aroused, encouraged and strengthened.

What does it involve? To get to know someone, you first need to be silent, to listen to what the other person has to say. You have to cultivate patience. You have to take your time. This prerequisite, obvious in theory, is not so obvious in practice. The Surabaya experience led me to live it, if only for a few days. There were many moments when I was baffled by what was said and explained. For example, I had no idea that a young female academic could chair our academic session at the Muslim university to which we were invited on the second morning, and give the floor to her male colleagues.

It is in conversation with others that I discover what I think, says the Master of the Order. The phrase can be frightening. Should I be malleable, suggestible, in the wrong sense of the word? Certainly not. It is about believing that the other person has something so essential to say to me, that my own thinking, my own logic, cannot be truly complete without the other person's word. Dialogue is self-fulfilment."

Zagreb, Croatia January 2016

It was snowing... An international colloquium, *Do religions have a significance for Europe?* was organised by the Croatian Dominicans and brilliantly led by brother Srecko Koralija, then Regent of Studies. This was an important step, as the colloquium brought together speakers from all the countries of the former Yugoslavia. The topics addressed included essential issues for the Church in the region, as well as politics, theology and public life. Marie Monnet contributed a publication. *Théologie implicite de l'intégration européenne* (Implicit Theology of European Integration). This is an opportunity to meet Professor Louis-Léon Christians, from UCLouvain, who is also a speaker.

Jerusalem, Israel-Palestine, July 2017

An "Archaeology and the Bible" session has been organised at the École Biblique et Archéologique Française de Jérusalem (EBAF), located near the Damascus Gate on the site where the first Christian martyr, Stephen, was stoned to death. The EBAF teachers were pleased to present their research to an informed audience, safe in the knowledge that they would not cause any scandal. Guided by Brother Dominique Marie Cabaret, the participants in the session went into the field to make archaeological discoveries in Jerusalem, Bethlehem, Galilee, Samaria and the Jordan Valley. In the vaulted rooms of the Bible en ses traditions (BEST, The Bible in its Traditions), Brother Olivier-Thomas Venard presented the research behind this ambitious programme, which uses computer and web resources to provide access to different Bible variants and interpretations. Nobody came back the same way they left.

Paris, , 20th anniversary on 16 May 2018

Just a stone's throw from the Élysée Palace, at 222 Boulevard Saint-Honoré, Domuni is celebrating its 20th anniversary. Videos are available on the public website, and here is the letter from Brother Bruno Cadoré, Master of the Order.

14/05/2018

Dear Brother Michel,

On the eve of the Domuni 20 celebrations, which are taking place in a few days' time, I am writing to you, of course, as the initiator of this adventure, but also to Brother Jean-Claude Lavigne, Sister Marie Monnet and Nicole Awaïs, who are carrying this project forward alongside you today. Thank you very much for your kind invitation to the meeting. Unfortunately, I am unable to attend as I am held back in Rome by the plenary session of the General Council. Please accept my apologies.

Twenty years already! That is both a lot and too little for such a project. And indeed a lot has been achieved in terms of the tenacity, organisational efforts, meetings and conversations that have taken place over the years to raise awareness of the project and convince people, which is not always easy when innovation is involved. A lot, too, thanks to the loyalty and expertise that they built up through the patient construction of networks, alliances and agreements. All of this has gradually established Domuni Universitas as not just an institution (which it unarguably is), but first and foremost as a network of trust, friendship, study, research, skills, cultures, innovation and professionalism. However, one may say it is still too little when you consider the success already achieved in just twenty years: the number of students who have found the path of study they were looking for at Domuni; the network of teachers and researchers who have agreed to contribute; and the other academic institutions that have formed deep ties with Domuni, one way or another. So, to us, this seems too little in the face of the long and bright future that we hope this online university will have.

The Order of Preachers can be particularly proud of this achievement. As a matter of fact, at a time of such decisive changes in communication and study methods, this project's founding idea proudly embodies essential elements of Dominic's *propositum*. The Domuni project is an initiative that seeks to reach individuals as closely as possible to their particular reality (culture, location, availability, prior training, desire for qualified study of the realities of faith, etc.), while also opening up to the universal, intercultural and cross-disciplinary dialogue and knowledge. Following in Dominic's footsteps, this project firmly establishes that study is one of the most effective ways of fostering a shared approach to thinking in pursuit of truth, grounded in the rigour and critical demands of tradition. The community of study and research promoted and established by Domuni Universitas is a sign of a unity that precedes us, but which we can nonetheless help to reveal, at the heart of the plurality of worlds and cultures. There are many similarities between Dominic's original intention in founding his Order and the work of Domuni Universitas, which is carried out day after day by everyone involved.

I wish to express my gratitude for all this, both personally and on behalf of the Order of Preachers. I am well aware that there is undoubtedly still much to be done in terms of organising institutional realities, consolidating academic excellence further, welcoming new students and recruiting new teachers and researchers, linking disciplines and cultures, and ensuring the necessary academic recognition. These are the tasks of those directly responsible, as well as the association that runs the university and the Order's provinces that support it. I assure you that, at a general level, the Order will always endeavour to provide the necessary support to ensure the project's full success, as it makes such a wonderful contribution to the Dominican adventure.

May the Lord, through the intercession of Saints Dominic, Albert the Great and Thomas Aquinas, and the many other saints of the Order who were sanctified by their search for truth, bless Domuni Universitas.

Once again, I express my admiration, gratitude and fraternal friendship.

Brother Bruno Cadoré, O.P., Master of the Order

Amman, Jordan. October 2018

A "Bible and Archaeology" session was organised at the invitation of N., whose family-in-law is Jordanian, her brother-in-law being Minister of Higher Education. A few days before departure, we learned that N. was not coming and that nothing had been planned. Our general secretary, Ms Clémentine Franchi, who has always handled difficult situations with calm determination, took charge of the logistics, including transport, accommodation, a guide and a travel agency. Brother Dominique Marie Cabaret from the EBAF was our guide, and Brother Ameer Jajé, who was in Jordan for a congress, was accompanying us. Having an Arab speaker who knew the country well made all the difference. After a long walk, which was sometimes vertiginous, we reached the summit of Petra to admire a city built entirely from hollows. For the descent, some of us were hoisted onto the backs of mules with more or less secure hooves – an experience that we will not forget anytime soon! In Madaba, we admired the mosaic depicting the Roman reconstruction of Jerusalem. In Kerak, we visited the Crusader fortress. On Mount Nebo, where Moses died after receiving a "kiss from God", we admired the Promised Land that he had only seen from afar. At Macheronte, we meditated on the death of John the Baptist. At Jerash, a complete Greco-Roman city opens up to visitors. At the ford of Penuel, on the torrent of the Yabock, Jacob told us about his hand-to-hand struggle with God before being named Israel and limping off yabbok-yacob, yabbok-yacob... All in all, a successful trip. This session enabled us to forge friendships that supported Domuni in its development, particularly with the Swiss: Jean Louis Meylan, Pascal Bregnard, Marie-Antoinette Lorwich, members of the Domuni Switzerland association.

DOMUNI, A COLLECTIVE ADVENTURE

A petition to the General Chapter, 2019

The Domuni Board had been informed by the Provincial of Belgium[110] that a petition signed by the Provincials of Toulouse (Brother Loïc Marie Lebot), France (Brother Michel Lachenaud) and Switzerland (Brother Guido Vergauwen) had been sent to the General Chapter.

Petition from the provincials of France and Switzerland

« The success of Domuni throughout the world attests to the very contemporary relevance of this project, which has been blossoming for twenty years at the heart of the Order's charism and mission.

The provinces of France and Toulouse are delighted with this success, congratulate its promoters and are more than ever keen to encourage its development. Since 2010-2011, they have been providing Domuni with statutory support on behalf of the Order, in particular through the presence of the two Prior Provincials and the two Regents of Studies on the Board of Directors of the Domuni association (France, Law of 1901) and through the presence of the Regents on the Academic Council. The Swiss Province is accompanying the quality assessment process initiated at civil level in 2017.

In recent years, the rapid growth in the number of students and courses on offer on every continent, as well as the agreements signed with other university institutions, has led to a proliferation of academic and administrative bodies for the governance of Domuni, far beyond the territory of the two provinces, particularly in Belgium, Spain, Italy and Switzerland.

This new situation, with its prospects for development throughout the world, poses serious challenges, particularly in terms of governance and ecclesial recognition, and entails an increased responsibility for the Order in the way it carries and supports Domuni. The Provinces of France, Toulouse and Switzerland, aware that they are no longer in a position to provide this support adequately, have asked for the creation of an Improvement Committee under the responsibility of the Master of the Order. The purpose of this Committee is to ensure the continuity of Domuni Universitas on the ecclesiastical and Dominican levels, as well as to continue its efforts to improve academic standards. »

---

[110] Brother Philippe Cochinaux, even though Domuni's offices were in his province, did not want to sign this petition and pointed out to the other provincials that they would do well to inform or consult the institution concerned.

The General Chapter of Biên Hoa responded very positively.

> **Acts of the 2019 General Chapter**
>
> *367. [GRATULATIO] We congratulate the leaders of DOMUNI Universitas for the considerable development of its online courses, offered in five languages, as well as for its financial autonomy. This innovative response to an apostolic, academic, theological and pastoral need deserves to be developed.*
>
> *368. [COMMENDATIO] We recommend that DOMUNI Universitas set up several courses (approximately 15 to 30 hours) of ongoing formation in the languages of the Order. The English version should be prepared in close collaboration with the Angelicum. This online material could also form part of the annual Dominican Renewal Programme.*
>
> *369. [COMMENDATIO] We recommend that DOMUNI Universitas regularly communicate its training programmes to the various entities of the Order so that they can disseminate them externally and use them for their own purposes.*
>
> *370. [COMMISSIO] We instruct the Master of the Order and the General Council to support DOMUNI Universitas by declaring this activity "Activity under the vigilance of the Master of the Order" for six years. This support will take the form of an improvement committee made up of experts. In dialogue with DOMUNI Universitas managers, the committee will use its proposals to help DOMUNI implement the academic criteria highlighted by the certification process undertaken in Switzerland, such as the establishment of a Scientific Council, the appointment of permanent professors, the development of research activities and the creation of a coherent curriculum.*

The pandemic: Covid-19

We have forgotten Covid-19, and the collective memory has erased this traumatic episode. The war in Ukraine, the attacks by Hamas and Israel's response in Gaza are all human in nature. The world is in a terrible state, as bad as ever. But this time, we cannot blame a virus – it is our own doing.

We have forgotten about the pandemic and returned to life as it was before. But *Domuni post-lockdown* is not the same as *Domuni pre-lockdown*, and our institution has undergone a metamorphosis.

The pandemic

Let us remember the official figures[111]. As small as these numbers may seem, they are still considerable: seven million deaths worldwide, one million one hundred and twenty-seven thousand in the USA, seven hundred thousand in Brazil, four hundred thousand in Russia, nearly two hundred thousand in France and thirty-five thousand in Belgium. Morgues were saturated, refrigerated lorries were requisitioned and burials had been banned due to the risk of contagion. We have forgotten.

It all began in Wuhan, at the end of 2019. The Chinese authorities were unable to quell the rumours. Finally, they imposed a drastic lockdown. But it was too late to stop the virus spreading: by January 2020, it had arrived in the Alps, at the aptly named *Contamines*. In Italy, the first wave overran hospitals. Very soon, more than ten million people in France were infected, and more than 600 died every day. Governments decreed strict lockdowns. People living in big cities fled to the countryside. Teleworking was imposed. Only ducks walked the pavements. The French could only go out for an hour within a kilometre of their home, provided they had a signed declaration in their pocket, specifying their address and the timing of their outing. Soon, they would be filling in a form on their smartphone instead; police squads would be roaming, on the lookout... And I would be inspected twice on unassuming and lonely country roads in the heart of France.

Universities, as well as primary and secondary schools were turning to distance learning in a hurry. In a hurry, and so in a mess, haphazardly transposing onto screens what was done in the classroom. Streaming is used, videoconferences are held, and work plans are sent out. An improvisation, a general "everyone for themselves". For almost two years, there was resentment against e-learning. Which was unfair, because it helped us to hold on in spite of everything. Admittedly, it was total improvisation. There was no time to think about the use of this new medium, which was unsuitable for 100% use in primary or secondary education, or for the very first years of university. We had to make do, and *make the best of a bad situation*.

---

[111] According to Statista, in August 2023.

One serious look at the number of confirmed cases and the sight of hastily built hospitals in China was enough for me to realise that, as the virus knew no borders, it would not be long before the scourge reached us. This was neither "just a bad flu" nor mass psychosis, as those around me kept saying.

In view of the bad news, we organised a crisis meeting to warn the Brussels international office employees: *You know the situation. It is evolving rapidly and we need to anticipate. When you leave this evening, take your laptop, power cable and hard drive with you. Plan ahead for possible teleworking. We will have a daily Zoom meeting from 11am to 12.30pm. Wait for our signal. If we give it, let us start this plan B.* The signal was sent over the weekend and, a fortnight later, the Belgian government imposed teleworking.

In Peru, I met an astonishing man, capable of turning problems into solutions. One example among many: as his citrus fruit trees were being attacked by butterflies, he covered them with large nets to protect not the citrus fruit but the butterflies, which he sold to tourists at a much higher price than his oranges and grapefruit.

In this spirit, Domuni has used confinement as a formidable incubator for innovation. The figures speak for themselves: 100% business growth by 2020, so much so that, in a recorded video conference, brother Guido Vergauwen mischievously wondered whether we might not have had something to do with the appearance of the virus. Does crime pay in the end?

In this case, distance learning was meeting a vital need. If you are stuck at home, you can still study, make the most of your time and get training. Enrolments were flooding in. A maximum number of grants were awarded, courses were offered free of charge and, even so, revenue rose by fifty per cent.

Work was plentiful. We needed to recruit, also remotely. Job interviews took place via Zoom. When we meet afterwards, we are surprised. The person I see is not the person I imagined, smaller or larger.

Unesco strongly encouraged distance learning[112]. Our institution fit the bill of the policy driven by the European Union[113] and devised by various research groups.

> **Paradoxical recognition**
>
> The main criterion is recognition by peers (peer review), which is difficult for newcomers, if not impossible in a competitive environment. That leaves recognition by the crooks. They have an astonishing flair for unearthing real value. With their boundless creativity, they are *wiser than the children of light*[114].
>
> A few professional bandits have paid tribute to our institution's teams in this way. At the beginning of September 2020, an American journalist contacted Carly Wood, the head of English training. Ben Wieder, a specialist in anti-corruption investigations, was concerned to know whether there was an institutional agreement between Domuni and AnnJose University in New Orleans. The answer was no, so he pointed us to an English-language sister site to ours, which had been copied to such an extent that the word Domuni still appeared on some pages.
>
> A similar case had already arisen and, to defend ourselves, we sent a file to Google asking it to stop referencing the plagiarist site. But this was worse than what we were used to. It was no longer just a case of tricking students into paying through a fraudulent account. As the journalist wrote in the *Miami Herald* on 9 September 2020, it was a case of cheating the State of Florida (!) out of loans granted to businesses to get through the health crisis. More than 3 million dollars had been paid to the ingenious swindlers.
>
> High-flying hackers have shown that even an American state recognises the seriousness of our university. By anticipating this possibility and choosing our site to commit their misdeed, should we not read, on their part, a tribute from vice to virtue?

---

[112] Audrey Azoulay, Director-General of Unesco, "La moitié des élèves et étudiants privés de leur établissement d'enseignement : l'UNESCO lance une coalition mondiale pour accélérer la mise en œuvre de l'enseignement à distance" (Half of Pupils and Students Deprived of Their Educational Institution: Unesco Launches a Global Coalition to Accelerate the Implementation of Distance Education), 18 March 2020, updated on 20 April 2023. [Online].

[113] European Commission, "Digital Education Action Plan (2021-2027)", updated on 23 November 2023. [Online].

[114] Lk 16:8.

All companies have experienced lockdowns, but not all have undergone such a metamorphosis. To explain this, we need to understand that our school was very positively exposed to the rapid changes that lockdowns required. By investing in distance learning from 1998 onwards and organising it around cyberspace, while viewing classroom teaching as supplementary to it rather than the other way around, Domuni created a culture that enabled it to implement lasting changes in these new conditions. Although face-to-face meetings, workshops, Journées d'Études Participatives (JEP, Participatory Study Days), summer universities and sessions with partners in Jerusalem, Jordan, etc. were all highly valued, putting them on hold did not have a significant impact on our business. We learned to adapt by using the new tools.

By a stroke of providential luck, Zoom and Teams appeared right at the start of Covid. Their quality represented a major leap forward compared with Skype. The incessant suspension of connections, crackling and breaks that had made communication uncertain and led us to choose the written word as our main medium were no longer an issue. The technology was now advanced enough to facilitate institutional or pedagogical meetings that were just as effective as face-to-face ones. We could record meetings, install simultaneous translation and share screens. This extended the available time in our diaries. There was no more wasted time travelling back and forth, and no more transport, accommodation or catering costs. Some may have missed the warmth of physical meetings. However, it was important to distinguish between objectives: a working meeting was not a social gathering, and there was nothing to stop us planning days of social interaction, with or without an agenda.

Following the lockdown, three days of face-to-face meetings were organised in Greece. Our many collaborators in Madrid, Baghdad, Beirut, Oslo, Brussels, Rome and Douai all came together in Athens. There is nothing quite like a pilgrimage to Delphi to discuss teaching philosophy. Similarly, there is nothing like an exchange on the ancient Agora to discuss the acculturation of the Christian faith. Face-to-face team meetings were then organised in Paris. Whenever one of us fell prey to Covid-19, the meeting was held in the open air in the Parc du Luxembourg – under the bandstand when it rained. Despite the lack of comfort, we got through this stressful period and it is good to have forgotten it!

We chose to continue teleworking, renouncing the model of centralised administration. None of us has ever regretted it. However, we had to adapt to employment legislation. As we were unable to pay salaries from France or Belgium to people working in Italy, Lebanon, the DRC, Norway and Spain, we asked our remote employees to become self-employed and invoice us at the end of the month. The network model was the obvious choice. Distance learning made the institution's organisational structure more accessible. The recruitment pool was no longer limited to a specific geographical area, but extended to the limits of cyberspace; i.e., the entire planet. It was at this point that I came up with the idea of university synergy: not just one networked university, but networked universities pooling their resources, including teachers, research, students and accreditations.

The breakdown: the OVH server fire on 11 March 2021

Pandemics are a rare threat, but breakdowns are not. Advanced technologies are vulnerable to bugs. The adjective "virtual" can give the misleading impression that we are beyond hardware, when in fact everything passes through matter. On Thursday, 11 March 2021, the OVH servers hosting Domuni's programmes caught fire in Strasbourg. Flames reaching 40 metres high engulfed buildings on the banks of the Rhine. Sixteen thousand customers were affected, most of whom lost everything. Our website was restored to its original state twelve hours later. Alan Rives, our Spanish IT engineer, informed us that he had set up an updated backup system in Roubaix at OVH. It was a close call, and the Spanish team responsible for security received warm congratulations. Since then, a third server has been installed in Madrid.

Distance can rhyme with chance

> *I am looking for the emergence of a presence,*
> *the excess of reality that ruins all definitions.*
>
> Christian Bobin[115]

For a theology of distance[116]

Innovative practice needs reflexivity. What are we doing? How can we explain the phenomena we observe? What does this new world we are discovering mean? How does this affect our understanding of faith? How does the daily practice of distance teaching affect my theology? In Appendix 4, I answer the questions posed by the journal Noosphère, from a Teilhardian perspective. Here, I simply re-read a few passages from the Gospel.

Jesus is both close and distant

He makes forbidden contacts. He touches the leper[117], and this is forbidden under the law of ritual purity. In the same way, he drinks the water of the Samaritan woman, he lets himself be touched by the prostitute[118], by the woman with haemorrhoids[119]. He touches the

---

[115] Christian Bobin, *Pierre,* Paris, Folio, 2021, p 9.

[116] It was at the behest of Brother Franklin Buitrago, O.P., Dean of the Faculty of Theology at the University of Santo Tomas de Aquino (USTA), in Colombia, for a colloquium that was partly in person and partly remote in November 2021, that I felt compelled to delve more profoundly into this experience.

[117] Mt 8:3.

[118] Lk 7:38.

[119] Mt 9:20.

little girl who is said to be dead[120]. He eats at the table of sinners[121]. He washes the feet of his disciples[122]. He then gets too close, transgressing the established boundaries.

In contrast, Jesus is absent when we want him to be present. He remained at a distance when he learned that his friend Lazarus was ill. Mary and Martha criticised him for this, saying that it showed a lack of faithfulness in friendship. *Lord, if Thou hadst been here, my brother would not have died*[123].

Distance comes with delay. For Lazarus, the absence lasted three days, alluding to Passover. This is similar to when Jesus' parents lost their child before finding him. The theme of delay is common in the Bible: *When will you come?* Presence is an object of hope: it is deferred, it calls for trust. Absence is measured in terms of days, years, centuries, rather than kilometres.

Jesus is not where we expect him to be; he appears where we least expect it. *Let us go into the next towns!*[124] You cannot hold him back, *Touch Me not*[125], you cannot lay a hand on him. This distance is a sign of freedom, a freedom that disturbs us because it causes frustration. It is similar to the question put to God throughout the Bible: *Where are you?* Which, in the 19th century, came to be expressed by the majority of Europeans in this accentuated form: Does God exist? In the gospel parables, God is compared to a great landowner who has gone away. He has distributed his goods (the talents[126]) or entrusted his vineyard (the murderous vinedressers[127]). He has left and he is coming back. Philosophers describe him as both transcendent and immanent. He calls himself imminent: *Be vigilant*!

Putting a place into perspective means putting into perspective many of the things involved in geographical location. We see this in

---

[120] Lk 8:54.
[121] Mk 2:15.
[122] Jn 13:8.
[123] Jn 11:20.
[124] Mk 1:38.
[125] Jn 20:17.
[126] Mt 25:14.
[127] Mt 21:33.

Jesus' dialogue with the Samaritan woman. Place is erased in favour of interiority: *[...] Ye shall neither on this mountain, nor yet at Jerusalem, worship the Father [...] but in spirit and in truth*[128]. Neither there nor elsewhere: with the heart. As a result, religions, with their set of rites, their clergy, their multiple cultural references, are put into perspective: it is a question of worshipping *in spirit and in truth*, we would say today *with the heart*. That is where true presence lies: *Abide in Me, and I in you*[129]. *Suffer little children, and forbid them not to come unto Me*[130]. To abide is to love. *For where two or three are gathered together in My name, there am I in the midst of them*[131]. Where is he? Wherever love is present. *Ubi caritas est vera, Deus ibi est*. It is a place that cannot be identified geographically, a presence that cannot be located.

There is no longer an *omphalos* – the centre or navel of the world, as claimed by Delphi in Greece, or Cusco in Peru (*el ombligo del mundo*). The centre is everywhere and, in the Apocalypse, there is no longer a Temple[132]. The peripheries are no longer despised: *Can any good thing come out of Nazareth?*[133] There is no more talk of Rome or Jerusalem: *And they shall say to you, "See, here!" or "See, there!" Go not after them, nor follow them*[134]. *God is an infinite sphere, the center of which is everywhere, the circumference nowhere*[135]. On the other hand, you must go to the people, for it is among them that you will meet him: *He goeth before you into Galilee*[136], that is, *the land of Zebulun and the land of Naphtali, by the way of the sea, beyond the Jordan, Galilee of the Gentiles*[137]. *Go ye therefore and teach all nations*[138]. He seeks to gather them *even*

---

[128] Jn 4:21-23.

[129] Jn 15:4.

[130] Mt 19:14.

[131] Mt 18:20.

[132] Rev 21:22.

[133] Jn 1:46.

[134] Lk 17:23.

[135] Pascal Blaise *Pensées* (Thoughts) 198, Lafuma, Brunschvicg 383.

[136] Mt 28:7.

[137] Mt 4:15.

[138] Mt 28:19.

as a hen gathereth her chickens under her wings[139]. Their dispersion moves him to the point of making him weep[140].

As with the agony and the cross, the accounts of the deserted tomb are the most obvious experience of God's absence. They are well worth meditating on.

In Mk 16:5 and Mt 28:1-10, the tomb is not empty, since a young man dressed in white says: *He is not here*. He is no longer where they put him, he is somewhere else. *And entering into the sepulcher, they saw a young man sitting on the right side, clothed in a long white garment; and they were frightened. And he said unto them, "Be not afraid. Ye seek Jesus of Nazareth, who was crucified. He is risen! He is not here. Behold the place where they laid Him. But go your way. Tell His disciples and Peter that He goeth before you into Galilee. There shall ye see Him, as He said unto you."*

In Luke 24, two mysterious men testify that we must not look for the living One among the dead. *Now upon the first day of the week very early in the morning, they came unto the sepulcher, bringing the spices which they had prepared; and certain others were with them. And they found the stone rolled away from the sepulcher. And they entered in and found not the body of the Lord Jesus. And it came to pass, as they were much perplexed about this, behold, two men stood by them in shining garments. And as they were afraid and bowed down their faces to the earth, they said unto them, "Why seek ye the living among the dead? He is not here, but is risen!"*

In John 20, clues – a form of order in the linen cloths, laid flat, and the shroud, rolled up separately – help *the disciple whom Jesus loved* to understand Scripture. *He saw, and believed*. He did not see what he believed. *Peter therefore went forth, and that other disciple, and came to the sepulcher. And they both ran together, and the other disciple outran Peter and came first to the sepulcher. And stooping down and looking in, he saw the linen cloths lying, yet he went not in. Then came Simon Peter following him, and went into the sepulcher and saw the linen cloths as they lay and the napkin that had been about His head, not lying with the linen cloths, but wrapped*

---

[139] Mt 23:37.
[140] Lk 19:41.

together in a place by itself. Then the other disciple, who came first to the sepulcher, went in also; and he saw, and believed. For as yet they knew not the Scripture, that He must rise again from the dead.

The absence of the body in the tomb raises a question, a question that has no obvious answer, but which points to a message. On the evening of the first day of the week, the Risen One breaks in. Each time, the evangelist points out that the doors were *locked* (Jn 19:26). It was an excess of presence. The disciples are *filled with joy*. But the last words of Jesus, in John's Gospel, call us to believe without physical evidence, to believe in spite of absence: *Because thou hast seen Me, thou hast believed. Blessed are they that have not seen and yet have believed.* (Jn 20:29).

Jesus mediates and teaches from a distance

In the Jewish and Christian faith, there are always many mediations, and their fragility has an important significance. Enraged by the sight of the golden calf, Moses on Sinai, for example, smashed the Tablets of the Law[141]. This indicates that neither the symbol of fertility nor the Tablets of the Law written by God's very hand (the following being written by men) should be viewed as absolute, which is contrary to how Muslims perceive the Koran[142].

Let us go deeper. When I teach online, the distance between me and the student pales in comparison to the distance between me and the person I am talking about. I am not Christ, but his servant – useless though I may be, I am still his servant! Jesus takes the risk of delegation in full awareness. It was to Peter, who had denied him, that he said: *Feed My lambs*. It was to Paul, who had persecuted him, that he entrusted the evangelisation of non-Jews[143]. The distance between the messenger and the one to whom he bears witness is immense; it is such an abyss that this "glaring" gap carries a meaning that it is imperative to meditate on.

---

[141] Ex. 32:19.

[142] Cf. F. Nietzsche's comments on this subject by Jean-Luc Marion in *L'Idole et la distance* (The Idol and Distance), 1977.

[143] "*I am Jesus whom thou persecutest.*"

The Risen One does not write or speak directly. By deliberate choice, he communicates through his disciples. This very important fact teaches us many things. The disciples themselves, like Saint Paul, will send epistles, which means that they will not be present in the community to which they are addressed. Paradoxically, this distance allows us today to be recipients in our turn and to enter into this apostle-disciple relationship by reading with them what is intended for them.

The medium is the message![144] The message is powerful, but the medium is fragile: it appears to have been chosen for this very reason. Faith is proposed, not imposed. To announce his resurrection, Jesus chose Mary Magdalene: a woman; a layperson; and a repentant sinner. This tells us a lot. Christ chose a despised medium. Why did he do this? Because the medium is in tune with the discreet message, which does not impose itself but is offered softly and is far removed from triumphalism. *He that is able to receive it, let him receive it.*[145]

In the Gospel, Jesus shows rather than tells. Rather than explaining, he acts. To teach theology, faith must first be awakened, the faith of the student and also the faith of the teacher[146].

Near Capernaum, Jesus taught from a boat, across the water[147]. Nothing of his teaching is transmitted. Could this be because the disciples retained nothing? It seems that the way in which the teaching is transmitted, the medium, is more important than the content or message itself.

This story reveals a structure, a pattern, a theological logic. Jesus teaches from the lake to the multitude on the shore. Between the two there is water. This Gospel is topical; what it says is still true. Jesus not only teaches with words, that is to say from a distance, but he also teaches from the water, that is to say, in the biblical symbolism, beyond death, because water, as in baptism, is a symbol of death.

---

[144] *The medium is the message* is a phrase emblematic of Marshall McLuhan's thinking.
[145] Mt 19:12.
[146] See Paul Ricœur's article in *Lectures 3 (Readings 3)*, on the hermeneutics of witness.
[147] Mk 4:1; Lk 5:1-11.

The Risen One teaches the Church from beyond death. It is a presence at the heart of absence: a presence at a distance, an absence inhabited by a certain presence, perceptible through faith.

Jesus heals from a distance

The centurion of Capernaum[148] sends emissaries to tell Jesus that he needs his help, and that Jesus does not need to go anywhere. He himself stood at a distance from Jesus and encouraged him to intervene from afar. *And Jesus went with them. And when He was not far from the house, the centurion sent friends to Him, saying unto Him, "Lord, trouble not Thyself, for I am not worthy that Thou shouldest enter under my roof. Therefore neither thought I myself worthy to come unto Thee. But say the word, and my servant shall be healed."*

This acceptance of distance marks the power of his faith: *When Jesus heard these things, He marveled at him, and turned about and said unto the people who followed Him, "I say unto you, I have not found so great a faith, no, not in Israel."*. This was, in passing, a scandalous remark since the centurion was not Jewish, but Roman. Could it have been a way of announcing the conversion of pagans and the universality of salvation?

In Luke's Gospel, Jesus heals ten lepers[149] on the road without touching them, and with a delayed effect. Only one of them turns around and returns to thank Jesus. He realises that he owes Jesus something "in return"; he is grateful. Here, the rediscovered presence comes from recognition.

In Mark's Gospel, Jesus establishes physical contact with a leper[150], which was forbidden by the Law for reasons of ritual impurity. Even though he had cured the leper, and therefore the contagion had gone from health to disease and not from the sick person to the one who touched him, Jesus still had to move away. It was as if he had been socially, rather than medically, contaminated, as if he had *taken the sin upon himself.* After the leper was healed, Jesus had to avoid the villages and stand aside like an outcast. Their

---

[148] Lk 7:1-10.
[149] Lk 17:11-19.
[150] Mk 1:45.

situations have effectively been exchanged. Jesus is expelled because he draws close to those who are excluded, with the intention of reintegrating them. We see this phenomenon again with the possessed man of Gerasa[151] and the meal shared by Matthew[152], among others.

In the Gospel of John, Jesus heals a man who was born blind. He touches him by putting saliva on his eyes. Once again, the healing is delayed; it only occurs after the blind man takes Jesus at his word and goes to the Pool of Siloam to wash and be healed. Jesus' presence when he touched the man did not produce the light of the encounter immediately. The real encounter takes place after the healing, and, above all, after the formerly blind man undergoes a trial and is expelled, in preparation for the trial of Jesus. This enables the healed blind man to encounter Christ outside the city in an Easter apparition.

Jesus accompanies at a distance

Terrified by the waves and wind, the disciples face a storm at night. Jesus appears to them, walking on water and approaching them from a distance. According to the Gospels of Mark and Matthew (14:22-33), the storm calms down when he climbs aboard. In John's Gospel (6:15-21), when Jesus enters the boat, they reach land, signifying the conclusion of the journey and the union of Jesus and the Church.

In theology, as in many other disciplines, distance is a journey, so it takes time. There is no such thing as space *and* time, only space-time. Space is equivalent to a certain amount of time and can be converted into walking time. Conversely, time can be understood as the distance travelled. There is a distance in time. Absence often means "not yet"; being far away means "a long time from now"; being near means "soon"; presence means "arrival", "now". From the perspective of a journey, reaching the end of the road marks the conclusion of the journey and the story. Therefore, distance is a positive element because it allows us to move forward and gives us time. Conversely, presence kills time. More precisely, when we are

---

[151] Mk 5:17.
[152] Mt 9:9.

present, time no longer offers space for progression; it is fulfilled as a pleroma, a quality of eternity and a quantity of non-eternity (Hegel's bad infinity). From a pedagogical point of view, arrival provides evidence and knowledge – or rather, intuition – the light that springs to the mind or heart. Love is presence and immediacy. Conversely, desire, like the question, is space because it is a delay to be filled before satiation.

For dialogue to be possible, a certain distance is necessary between two people. An embrace is not conducive to wide-ranging discussions, nor is full agreement. Between a learner and a teacher, a space is essential, as is a delay between words and their reception. There should also be a repetition of encounters spaced out over time to allow for assimilation and reflection. This is how it is between lovers. Paradoxically, we can regret that the long delays between writing and receiving an actual letter, with ink and paper, have come to an end.

In this epistolary exchange, a relationship matured that electronic messages, which are too quick, cannot build to the same depth, even if they are more intense because we can hear and see each other. We have never understood so well before what is wrong with the fusion of immediacy. There is something violent here, and encounters between religions – between mystics, therefore – whether spousal (often Christian) or fusional (often Eastern or Muslim), will show this more and more clearly. In essence, when I consider myself to be God, when I identify with him or merge with him[153], seemingly alone and self-sufficient, I am at high risk of becoming totalitarian and violent.

So we understand: space or time is life, just like growth (quantitative) and development (qualitative); whereas the here and now, without any movement or change, is psychic death.

Death, however, is an opening towards nothingness or towards the afterlife, another form of life. Death becomes the ultimate space to cross, and thus the paradigm of all space.

---

[153] As when Saint Paul wrote: *I am crucified with Christ, nevertheless I live; yet not I, but Christ liveth in me.* (Ga 2:20)

No one can see God without dying. This is even more true in the sense that no one can see God without suffering and experiencing the Passover of dispossession: the loss of the self through the self, and resurrection through the Other. We then enter the realm beyond time and reach the other shore. Even better, we reach the summit of the transfiguration mountain. These eternal moments can pierce life, and it is imperative that we descend from these summits so that all that they signify can be fulfilled in concrete history. Death becomes an analogy for any transformation.

In this beautiful expression, *to leave is to die a little*, space is surreptitiously reintroduced. To die is also to leave.

Distance is necessary: *Verily I say unto you, no prophet is accepted in his own country*[154]. Witnesses must come from elsewhere. Distance is a form of transcendence. Jesus himself said that he had to leave so that his disciples could grow in strength. *Nevertheless I tell you the truth. It is expedient for you that I go away, for if I go not away, the Comforter will not come unto you; but if I depart, I will send Him unto you*[155].

The Samaritan approaches the almost dead man and touches him to heal his wounds[156]. This is true. But once the wounded man has been handed over to the innkeeper, the benefactor pays for the stay and leaves. He does not do everything, he delegates the rest, and distances himself to live his own life.

The rescued man must love the person who *became his neighbour* and saved him without imposing their benevolent presence, because they left. Distance is the condition of faith because it fosters freedom.

Sometimes, absence is doubled. When the women run to the tomb, they hope to find a corpse, but even that is denied them! *He is not here. Behold the place where they laid Him*[157]. This statement

---

[154] Lk 4:24.
[155] Jn 16:6-7.
[156] Lk 10:34.
[157] Mt 28:6; Mk 16:6.

applies to many things, liturgical habits, certain dogmatic formulas... Jesus, to say the least, does not spare his disciples from trauma.

The last sentence of the Gospel according to Matthew, at the moment of Jesus' departure, is a major paradox: *And lo, I am with you always, even unto the end of the world.* He is *with* us, but he is leaving. He is with us, but at a distance. Love creates distance to bring us together. *As the Father hath loved Me, so have I loved you... As My Father hath sent Me, even so send I you.* In a surge of love, the Father sends his Son, who in turn sends his disciples, so that they may all be one.

Jesus teaches from a distance, and this is not an obstacle; it is a choice he made himself. Distance corresponds to the essence and truth of what is at stake: faith. It is consistent with what needs to be taught and practised. The objective is the personal interiorisation of a message that cannot be taken for granted and that must be discovered and verified by putting it into practice. The objective is to awaken a conviction without proof, immediate verification or constraint. *Now faith is the substance of things hoped for, the evidence of things not seen*[158].

It is not just an intellectual message, it is a way of life. It is said of Moses that *he endured as seeing Him who is invisible*[159]. The "distance" is based on this *as if: as if he saw*, without seeing directly, because it has not happened yet.

Real presence or real absence? We can ask ourselves this question: *For where two or three are gathered together in My name, there am I in the midst of them*[160]. Present in the icons, as with the Orthodox? In the biblical sharing, as with the Protestants? Not "in" the consecrated host, which would constitute "impanation", but in the shared bread and wine themselves, which have become his body and blood, as with Catholics? If we follow the invitation, *Become what you receive*[161], the distance is abolished. But is it a presence? *I am Jesus*

---

[158] Heb 11:1
[159] Heb 11:27.
[160] Mt 18:20.
[161] Saint Augustine.

whom thou persecutest[162] is an identification *Verily I say unto you, inasmuch as ye have done it unto one of the least of these My brethren, ye have done it unto Me*[163]. Presence or representation in the sense of the function of re-presenting? These two words come from the same root. Could the re-presentation be a redoubled presence?

The profound mystery of a raw presence and internalised communion, so strong that it leads to identification. Catholics who follow the ciborium and bow before the Blessed Sacrament should also bow before those who have just received Holy Communion, because this is the ultimate purpose of the sacrament: to make us members of the living body of Christ. Here, the words "presence" and "absence" are inadequate. The poet transcends these concepts. *I am looking for the emergence of a presence; the excess of reality that defies definition.* The poet challenges the intelligence of the theologian to consider this unique relationship, which is both transcendent and imminent.

Diversification and autonomy

Faith is not expressed in words alone; museums are full of religious works that bear witness to an implicit theology well worth studying. *I am going to give my catechism class*, said an agnostic friend of mine, a professor of art history in Montpellier. Quite naturally, our university set up a course in art history, which has grown to become a department. The Apostle Saint James wrote that a living faith is recognised by the actions taken, so it is only natural that our institution should be interested in human rights, ecology, the economy, management and spirituality, and that it should ask itself questions about other religions and the significance of religious diversity, as well as inter- and intra-religious dialogue, which lie at the heart of the spiritual experience. This list of teaching areas is enough to explain why Domuni can no longer have its administrative office in a convent, which would simply not be big enough.

---

[162] Ac 9:5; 22:8.

[163] Mt 25.

Following the metaphor of the pregnant woman, after a while the baby has to develop outside!

Lockdowns were a revelation in that they gave autonomy to heterogeneous dynamics. On the one hand, the convents were closed, but on the other, our school's staff were given all the tools they needed to continue their work from home: storage spaces for personal data, online meeting and discussion areas, archives of all kinds on Moodle, drives and Google for Education. Students and lecturers formed a highly available network supported by the administration, who were also working from home. One thing was clear: the location of the office no longer mattered. The problem had solved itself! However, there was still the question of what to do with the books and institutional, accounting and academic archives (assignments, exams, dissertations and student documents), as well as a small stock of dormant tools such as printers, scanners, large screens, staplers, files and paper in Brussels. I only became aware of this once the other collaborators had already understood it, and a coherent policy could be decided upon.

We had to find a location for the office, if possible a central one, and Paris was chosen. We organised ourselves into a small commando to visit a dozen possible locations. The driver remained in the vehicle while two of our team went to scout out the office. If the answer was positive, they called the driver, who parked the car for a few minutes while they went up to take a look. After an exchange of views, a final choice was made. A few weeks later, the office was set up in a wonderful location. The building is close to a metro station, a railway station, and the Boulevard Périphérique. Facing one of the capital's largest green spaces, which contains several thousand trees, it offers views of both the Montparnasse Tower and the Eiffel Tower. The neighbours are very quiet and include some great personalities: Baudelaire, Jean Paul Sartre and Simone de Beauvoir, Jacques Chirac, César Vallejo, Marguerite Duras... Recently joined by Elkabbach. Perhaps they inspired us discreetly?

Archives and equipment were transported back and forth to Brussels. Domuni was no longer rooted in a convent. On 1 September 2023, I retired as Rector. For the first time, the university was assuming its full autonomy, with no regrets. Nomadic and happy to be so, a citizen of the world.

Facilitating the network: face-to-face visits

In order to establish a network and bring our activities to life, the heads of our institution visited our Italian partners in Rome, Florence, Pistoia and Bologna, our Spanish partners in Madrid, Salamanca, Seville and Valencia, our Irish partners in Dublin and our biblical partners in Jerusalem. Sometimes they travelled in groups led by the General Secretary. There have also been trips further afield.

Canada, September 2012

A meeting with Dominican friars was organised in Montreal and Ottawa as part of the agreement signed with the Dominican College. The purpose of the trip was to look for collaborations for teaching in English. Gaston Raymond, Maxime Allard, Hervé Tremblay, Martin Lavoie and Darren Dias taught core courses for the bachelor's degree.

South Africa, Easter 2019

Brothers Philippe Denis, Stan Muyebe and Isaac Mutelo have entrusted some courses and promised others, which have not failed to arrive. An agreement was signed with the Dominican Vicariate and a magazine in English was launched.

Athens, 4-7 October 2021

After months of daily meetings by zoom, a face-to-face meeting of the international team was organised in Greece. The programme was packed with activities, including a visit to the Acropolis, a group photo, fine dining in the old quarter of the capital, a visit to Delphi in memory of the Pythia's oracle to Socrates, and a boat trip to the islands of Hydra, Poros and Aegina. The reunion strengthened our interpersonal connections and re-energised us all.

DISTANCE CAN RHYME WITH CHANCE

Iraq and Kurdistan, February 2022

At 5am in Erbil, the chant of the muezzin is heard in chorus from the surrounding mosques. Daybreak reveals a countryside eaten away at by more or less finished, elegant and ambitious buildings, with wide avenues whose double lanes are not yet asphalted. Here, people think big, with obvious optimism. Wealth is evident. The flares spotted from the plane in the night explain why. You only have to scratch the ground to find oil, which is impressive for those of us suffering from rising energy prices.

We were welcomed at the Catholic University of Erbil (CUE), brother Ameer Jajé, sister Marie Monnet and myself, all three dressed in the Dominican habit. This small university is a seed that promises to grow rapidly, just like everything else around it. You can feel the 21st century here: the computerisation, the English with its American influences, the young managers, the open-mindedness, the joy of living and working, the desire to take on new projects and the confidence to succeed. We have come for the symposium starting tomorrow, which is also an opportunity to sign a Memorandum of Understanding, as we will be doing with the University of Baghdad. We already share professors, including sisters who are doctors in various disciplines, as well as administrative staff, since several of their members are brothers, including two bishops.

Erbil is one of the world's oldest cities, dominated by a fortress on a rocky outcrop. Around the citadel, life bustles in the souks, where I buy something to protect myself from the cold.

The next morning, we attend the symposium on religious freedom in the conference room. After passing through the security checkpoint and completing the administrative registration, I am seated in the front row. *Everything is in order*, say the vice-chancellor and vice-rector behind me. An official has just entered and the people have stood up. Sitting on my left, he is hounded by photographers. The simultaneous translation works: Kurdish and Arabic, which everyone here understands, as well as English.

The opening speech begins with the ritual formula *In the name of Allah, the Most Gracious, the Most Merciful...* and immediately it is our turn. We have half an hour. Ameer takes over from me, in

Arabic, and then the questions come for both of us. A mullah dressed in traditional attire, whose ten-year-old son religiously greets me with a moving familiarity every time we meet, asks me a long-winded question that the chairman asks to be clarified. I answer based on my understanding. Ameer takes over for the next questions. Our contributions are well received. The fact that there are two of us is unique, if I may say so, and it seems to me that our delegation is balanced, with two men and one woman all wearing Dominican attire. It is a pity that Marie Monnet does not speak, as she usually does. During the break, we exchange business cards and get to know the other speakers.

Lunch is an array of dishes, each more delicious than the last. The students surround us. We start thinking about organising a two-part study trip to Paris and Erbil, to enable students to exchange ideas. The participants include Shia and Sunni Muslims, Yazidis and Christians of various denominations.

In the afternoon, communication resume. The debates become heated and passionate. People start raising their voices, the translators can no longer keep up and the speakers start talking over each other. I plug one ear with my thumb to focus on the earphone in the other ear. I am missing a lot. It is complicated... The question is blunt: *Should anyone who changes religion be killed? Should we not ask parliament to pass a law? We are in the 21st century and we cannot carry on with rules from another era.* Should the security service at the entrance to the university (there are two or three Americans we want to protect) not move inside to intervene? Fortunately, we are among intellectuals and I am reassured to see them finally shake hands. We spend the evening "debriefing", as they say today, in the French restaurant *Au déjà vu*.

Mosul, Thursday 17

The next day, we set off for Mosul, 77 km away, in Ameer's niece's car. We are still wearing the Dominican habit because, according to Ameer, this makes us easier to spot and safer. In fact, at the various checkpoints between Kurdistan and the part of Iraq controlled by the government, we pass through without presenting any documents whatsoever! Strangely enough, our identity as religious Christians is proving to be a passport.

The plain is dry. On the outskirts of Mosul, we start to see collapsed buildings and others that had been rebuilt. All the buildings are made of breeze blocks. The general impression is one of chaos, precariousness and dirt. Empty plastic bags flutter in the wind. The roadside is lined with countless garages housing wrecked vehicles. Congestion is everywhere.

The city centre is no different, consisting of low-rise buildings and a field of ruins. We are approaching two emblematic monuments that are currently being restored under the guidance of UNESCO: the mosque with the famous sloping minaret, from which the Daesh caliphate was proclaimed; and the "Church of the Hour", the Dominican convent. Brother Olivier Poquillon welcomes us and joins us with a group of visitors, including French, Italian and Canadian tourists, as well as UNESCO architects and journalists. We take photos to help us understand the buildings better, and the pace is brisk.

Declared a historic monument before the war, the convent was protected from the international coalition's missiles, which is why Daesh used it as a court, detention and torture centre. Next to it is a building known as the *prayer school*, where the small shoes of women and children were found. The damage was extensive, but the convent's general structure held together. The site had to be cleared of mines, unexploded rockets and rubble. Restoration work could now begin. Brother Olivier Poquillon, who is in charge, is impatient. It is a great joy to have him back. Unesco, funded by the United Arab Emirates, wants to rebuild the two buildings and symbolically form *a cultural bridge* over past conflicts. Historical manuscripts from the convent's library, in Syriac and other languages, were evacuated to Erbil a few days before the arrival of Daesh. But the books were burnt[164].

---

[164] One of them was mine, *Quand Dieu nous surprend* (When God Surprises us), as Brother Philippe Koshaba, who has since received the digital version, later told me.

Qaraqosh

We leave the convent and head for Qaraqosh, home to 40,000 people before Daesh, 20,000 of whom have now returned, almost all of them Christians. They all fled to Kurdistan in a matter of minutes. Their houses have been destroyed or burnt down. Not all of them have been restored, but the town has a clean and organised appearance that contrasts with Mosul.

We meet the Iraqi Dominican Sisters of Saint Catherine, a major local institution with several impressive buildings, including a primary school, a secondary school and a convent. It is moving to meet them again and speak French, exchanging news. Sister Marianne Goffoël, the Superior General of the Fichermont Congregation to which Sister Marie Monnet belongs, lived with them for over twenty years. The alumni have nothing but praise for them.

For my part, I got to know Brother Jean Marie Mérigoux, who lived here and published several books, including *Viens à Ninive* (Come to Nineveh). Jean Marie was always friendly, attending the summer universities and delivering specialised Domuni courses on the Middle East. His memory remains quite vivid.

As we walk through the village, Ameer shows us the house where he was born. We then move on to Qaraqosh's old town, where a museum is housed in ancient dwellings, some of which are troglodytic. The museum displays ancient objects ranging from farming implements and old irons to traditional clothing, as well as some of the first radio and television sets. The hosts, dressed in period costume, give us a warm welcome. We have our pictures taken and, a few days later, even appear on TikTok!

After visiting the beautiful Church of Saint John, where Pope Francis celebrated mass, we meet Brother Ameer's niece in her house with her husband, Rami. Also present are her uncle, a Monsignor, who was wearing a large pectoral cross, and her daughter and son. The eldest son is named after Uncle Noël and the youngest after our Brother Ameer. The little girl is very talented and excels at creating short TV programmes, presenting themes like a true professional. Being invited into a family is an invaluable gift for a foreigner. There is much laughter and joy, and we deeply enjoy this human moment, savouring fruit and a variety of cakes with coffee.

Back in Erbil

The sisters of Saint Catherine welcome us for lunch. We are all over the moon, and the food is as plentiful as it is delicious. Two sisters who are doctors of theology teach Arabic at Domuni. It was moving to meet each other "in person" and exchange ideas in English.

The Iraqi brothers belong to the Dominican Province of France (Paris). It was a pure joy to meet them in their convent and get to know the younger ones. We also meet Domuni students from the Mosul and Erbil regions who study Arabic, and talk to them about the difficulties they face. The administration of the Arabic section is not yet fully up to scratch, and some forums are missing... Something we would have to rectify. They appreciate the accessibility. We discover their diversity: one of them has *Muslim* written on his identity card, another is Yazidi, a third is Chaldean, and there is a nun. A mother who is a chemist in a a medical laboratory is also present.

Mgr Joussef Mirkis, the Chaldean archbishop of Kirkuk and an old Dominican friend, makes an appearance at the café. We are the same age. He is the founder of Bagdad Academy, with which Domuni has signed an agreement – which Ameer has put into practice by developing the Arabic part. We listen to his wise remarks: *Where there is vision, there is money. But where there is money, there is not necessarily vision.* This is how he was able to build a clinic for Alzheimer's patients in his diocese – an achievement he is very proud of. A priest accompanies him, dressed in a charcoal-coloured clerical robe like his own. Marie Monnet speaks to him in French and discovers that he is a grandfather to several grandchildren. In fact, Chaldean priests can be chosen from among married men. Soon, we pick up our luggage and head for Erbil International Airport. On arrival in Baghdad, a friend of Ameer's is waiting for us to help with the formalities. We then arrive at the Brothers' convent in the vast city centre.

The next morning, we set off for Babylon, which is 130 km away. The road is monotonous, lined with unfinished buildings, garages and warehouses on either side. Plastic bags fly around and get stuck on our bonnet, forcing us to stop, which makes them fall off. We cannot compare, but it seems we are out of luck. There is no sun, and only about three drops rain on the windscreen. The wind sometimes picks up, kicking up the dust as if we were in a fog.

But finally, Babylon! We think of Nebuchadnezzar II and the deportation of the Jews in 597 BC, and again in 587 BC under King Zedekiah. We think of the prophet Daniel and his den of lions. We also remember Ezekiel's great prophecy about the dry bones. It applies to so many situations!

We also recall the lament in Revelation about the destruction of Babylon the Great. This text has since been transposed to Rome, New York, and many other proud cities by those who feel oppressed. The victory of the Persian Empire under Cyrus that allowed the return from exile in 538... We pass under the blue porch of the Gate of Ishtar, adorned with chimera-like creatures bearing eagle claws, lion's paws, bull's busts and snake's heads.

The originals are in the Baghdad Museum, the Louvre and Berlin. The monumental restorations carried out during Saddam Hussein's reign do not hide the historical foundations, where bricks marked with cuneiform inscriptions can still be seen. A huge lion, carved from a block of basalt, covers a warrior. Before leaving, we climb up to Saddam's castle to catch a glimpse of the river. It is a shame there is no museum there, and hardly any explanation or overview. After all, only around 10% of the site has been excavated.

On the way back, we celebrate the Eucharist in the friars' little church with some Dominican sisters, who invite us to come to their house for dinner the next day.

Bagdad by night

Three Dominican friars and a sister set off with four members of a family of friends to discover a cultural part of Baghdad, which is very lively at night. This is a street that has been restored to house bookshops and other cultural shops on the ground floor. The street is pedestrianised and a family population, with many young people, strolls there in complete tranquillity. *Baghdad lacks places to relax*, says Brother Zeyad Karakoshi, and this place is much appreciated.

The end of the street leads to the Tigris quay. There is an embarkation there for those who want to take a little boat tour, and we accept our friends' invitation. I will never again sing Psalm 136 on my zither without thinking about it: *By the rivers of Babylon, there we sat down; yea, we wept when we remembered Zion. We hung our harps upon the willows in the midst thereof.*

Among the shops, I come across one that sold all the gadgets you would find in a university, the things you put on the deans' desks, little flags, graduation caps, with that characteristic Anglo-Saxon square, and all the things you give to conference participants.

After Lauds, we drive to the National University of Baghdad, where the Dean of the Faculty of Arts is waiting for us. He receives us elegantly in his office, along with the former dean, a philosopher whom Ameer knows well, and the head of external relations, an archaeologist. The conversation is ceremonious. They introduce themselves and tell us how interested they are in our visit. I start by expressing my gratitude and saying how amazed I am to be welcomed to a university in a country that is home to the very origins of civilisation. After a coffee, waiters offer us cakes, which we barely touch, then water, then tea... and the conversation continues, Arabic-French, thanks to the simultaneous translation of Brother Ameer. He has had a migraine since he woke up, and I do not know how he can keep going for nearly three hours, looking as relaxed as ever. The points discussed are very concrete. They courteously warn us that the agreement cannot be signed for another three or six months, after it has been reviewed by various legal departments. Things are clear: teacher exchanges, joint study sessions, conferences and publications. We part with friendly gestures.

In the afternoon, in response to our request to walk around a bit, Brother Zeyad takes us on a tour of the neighbourhood. We pass the Nunciature and see the tarmac road that was paved for the Pope's visit. In our car tours, we pass several times by the square where students recently demonstrated against the regime. In a tunnel, large painted panels recall these events. The tower that the students had occupied is manned by a few soldiers. Things remain as they were.

My attention is drawn pilgrims carrying bundles, men among themselves, groups of women on their side, all dressed in black, black or red flags in their hands. At each stage, there are feeding places and a few mobile toilets. Brother Zeyad explains to me that this is a pilgrimage to the site of the martyrdom of the 12th disciple. The street is now packed with people. The shops on both sides are closed. It is popular and there is no clergy. People travel hundreds of kilometres for this mourning, travelling with virtually nothing. You can join in this collective mourning by helping the pilgrims with basic accommodation. Ameer tells me that as a child, he asked his parents why these people were still mourning someone who had died several centuries earlier. Since then, he has written his thesis on Shi'ism, and specifically on the place of suffering in the Ashura liturgy[165].

The bishop's residence is adjacent to the friars' convent. So we cross a few courtyards. Everything is newly built, clean and well kept. Ameer takes us on a tour of *Bagdad Academy*. We are impressed by the premises, which offer all the comfort and technology we could wish for: projectors connected to computers, comfortable lecture theatres, etc. Ameer welcomes us in his headmaster's office, next to the secretaries' and receptionists' offices. Our eyes go wide. We concelebrated with Mgr Jean, the Latin bishop of Iraq, of whom Ameer is vicar general (number 2). He is an affable Lebanese who speaks excellent French, and he introduces me to an Argentinian priest of Lebanese origin with whom I can converse in Spanish.

For dinner, we drive to the Iraqi Dominican sisters' house. Zeyad goes there on foot, but he insists that, for safety's sake, we go by car. The sisters are in charge of a maternity unit that "produces" around 500 babies a month. Everything is modern, clean and functional. Between this hospital and their neighbouring high school, which has 530 students aged 11 to 18 – 80% of them Muslim – are two Sisters' houses: one community for each of the works, because the rhythms are different. We are welcomed by all the sisters in a warm family atmosphere. I am trying to get to the bottom of this exceptional resilience. *We have no choice*, one of them tells me. *It is impossible without faith*, says another. Some speak French, others Italian or English. Most of their families have now moved abroad, to

---

[165] Available from Domuni-Press.

Europe, America or Australia. They remain, as they say, *missionaries in their own country*.

After Lauds, sung by the brothers in French every morning in the church, we set off for the national museum. Ameer, with his amazing network of contacts, has managed to get the museum – closed because of the pandemic – to open for us! It is simply incredible. One room follows another, and the lights come on as we walk along. Here and there, works damaged by vandals have been restored. As we walk among the masterpieces, the beauty rejuvenates us.

We celebrate Vespers and Mass in French with Brother Philippe Koshaba, who has just arrived from Mosul in a shared taxi – after sleeping his jet-lag off all morning. He shows us around the offices of *La Pensée Chrétienne* (Christian Thought), a magazine that has been published in Arabic for over 40 years. He presents us with his theology thesis, which he defended in Strasbourg, and we discuss the possibility of publishing it with Domuni-Press. As a publisher of Christian books, he explains the difficulties he faced during the embargo period and the current challenges of sending books by post to the diaspora. *Why not broadcast it digitally? We could take care of that*, we suggest.

Colombia and Peru, spring 2022

At the Santo Domingo convent in Bogotá, we are welcomed by around fifteen young Dominican students celebrating that month's birthdays. Here, we feel 'at home', somewhat disoriented by the 2,900-metre altitude and the New World. Built in the mid-20th century, the convent is made of brick and concrete. Perched on the heights of Bogotá, it neighbours a Dominican primary and secondary school with sports fields and classrooms. Across the road is another school, clearly high-end and bilingual, run by Dominican Sisters of the Présentation de Tours. This congregation was founded in France, but the sisters are Colombian.

In addition to Friar Franklin Buitrago Rojas, who teaches the students and is also dean of the Theology Faculty (having completed his doctorate at the University of Louvain), there is also a Colombian student friar who speaks good French. He spent time accompanying migrants with other young French Dominicans in Lille. There is also an Italian friar with us. He is working on his doctorate. The community is young and lively.

At breakfast, we are joined by a Dominican bishop emeritus. When we first arrived, Friar Franklin was our only reliable contact, but everything fell into place once we had settled in. Contacts were quickly made. Our first appointment was for Sunday morning over breakfast with the Dominican Dean of the Law Faculty in Tunja, Friar José Fernando Mancipe Giraldo, O.P., and then we went on to meet Professor Marisel Mena López, who had been recommended by Friar Franklin. I quickly sent a few emails and WhatsApp messages to arrange other meetings.

Marisel Mena López came to meet us at the convent. A doctor of biblical theology, she has over fifteen years' experience teaching and researching feminist interpretations of the Bible. Drawing on liberation theology, she is deeply rooted in the experience of often stigmatised Afro-Asian communities. Reconstruction is a recurring theme in our discussions, particularly in terms of rebuilding socio-cultural foundations based on biblical principles, such as the rules of the Sabbath. The professor completed a Master's degree in Angola, which has given her linguistic and cultural proficiency in Portuguese. Her research evaluates the impact of postcolonial readings in the biblical field, and she had just been awarded an honorary doctorate in the United States.

We discuss the UNESCO Chair project, in which she has shown a great deal of interest. For Marisel Mena López, the issue of acknowledgement, particularly with regard to black women, is a key area of research. Her work is based on fieldwork examining the displacement of black communities by violence. How can self-esteem be restored? How can we support legal procedures that can deliver justice for victims of rape? How can war crimes be condemned?

Marisel Mena López encourages 'folk readings' of the Bible and alternative projects, such as urban gardens, to promote 'living well' and engage with young people from diverse backgrounds. The professor promotes academic research based on tangible reality –a method which she humorously describes as undoubtedly more 'feminine' and which sometimes encounters 'resistance from theologians'.

The conversation concludes with the hope of establishing an active, research-based collaboration, which would be extremely fruitful. Marisel Mena Lopez has agreed to work with the Unesco Chair, an agreement she will confirm on Monday afternoon at the meeting with the Faculty of Theology. She will coordinate collaboration with Domuni on behalf of the faculty prior to the establishment of the Chair. In short, it was a wonderful meeting with an enthusiastic person to work with in the future.

In the afternoon, we toured Bogotá's historic centre, visiting the cathedral and five museums, including the Archaeological Museum and the Gold Museum. We also visited the Franciscan Church and the Church of Santa Clara. It rained, the wind blew and the cold chilled our bones. However, in the late afternoon, the sun came out and everything felt totally different.

Street art has developed significantly in Latin America, with guidebooks recommending a visit to Bogotá in particular for this reason! I took lots of photos and it was then that I came up with the idea of writing a course now entitled 'Engaged Art'.

After returning to the convent at the end of the afternoon, we shared a meal and continued our philosophical and theological discussion with Friar Adalberto Cardona Gómez. I first met him in July 1991 in Cuzco, where he was a teacher. I saw him again in Rome, where he was a professor at the Angelicum, and then in Bogotá, where he invited me, as regent of studies, to sign an agreement with Domuni. We met again in Rome for the Order's eighth centenary. In short, Adalberto is an old and dear friend, intelligent and full of humour, and it was a pleasure to meet him again.

We discuss Friar Adalberto's research into the theological writings of Xavier Zubiri (1898–1983), a 20th century Basque theologian who developed a theological approach based on concepts from Greek and Thomistic metaphysics. Friar Adalberto is offering a course or seminar on this topic. He puts us in touch with a philosophy professor, O.Y. Aparicio Gomez.

Oscar Yecid Aparicio Gómez has doctoral degrees in both philosophy and education. He is pleased to give us a sneak preview of his personal website, which highlights his various areas of expertise [166]. A specialist in Thomas Aquinas's metaphysical thought, he was Dean of the Faculty of Philosophy at the USTA in 2018 before specialising in the use of ICT for virtual education.

He gets to the heart of the matter by presenting us his tutorial-style videos on YouTube, which aim to introduce Spanish-speaking higher education teachers to distance learning. Alongside his academic expertise in philosophy and theology, he has established a company called Ed&TIC. Together with engineers and educationalists, they are developing a network of Latin American and Spanish universities to publish books and journals, as well as training teachers in distance learning techniques. He is particularly notable as the editor of the International Journal of Pedagogy and Educational Innovation (https://editic.net/ripie) and the International Journal of Theoretical and Practical Philosophy (https://riftp.editic.net). He also organises international conferences. This should provide many opportunities for collaboration.

On Sunday afternoon, we then met two communities of Dominican sisters from the *Congrégation de la Présentation de Tours*, whose members are particularly active in the field, running NGOs. The sisters historically founded a clinic 70 years ago, which has grown considerably and is now located in a middle-class neighbourhood. A community of Dominican nuns is situated on the fourth floor of the main building. On the opposite side of the road, in a large house, is a second community comprising two sisters in training, one of whom is completing her medical studies. They welcomed us royally, treating us to hot chocolate (Colombia is a major cocoa producer) and local specialities. We were also introduced to some typical Bogotá dishes, such as 'pan de yuca' (manioc).

Before that, we took the time to talk in depth about the work that a foundation run by two exceptional Dominican twin sisters (who look very much alike!) carries out in a Bogotá barrio (shanty town). One of them runs a counselling office, an informal place where she listens to anyone who needs it, from the doorman to the clinic director (!). She was previously a member of the General Council of International Dominican Sisters in Rome. Her sister is the superior of

---

[166] See http://oscaraparicio.org.

the community next door to the clinic. They can see and talk to each other from their respective windows!

On Monday morning, 2 May, we met Friar Jorge Ferdinando Rodríguez Ruiz, O.P. Having served as a local rector in various cities, he is now the vice-president of the Universidad Santo Tomás de Aquino (USTA) and is in charge of the distance learning section. The first impression is one of great resources. Compared with French universities, you feel as though you're well into the 21st century here, if not the 22nd!

The *Primer claustro universitario de Colombia*, also known as Santoto, is Colombia's leading university and is justifiably proud of this fact. The USTA has around ten branches in Bogotá and a presence in five other Colombian cities. The current distance learning building is considered too small, so a new one is being constructed. It will be equipped with all the necessary facilities: large screens, recording rooms and a TV studio.

As we wanted to travel light, we didn't bring any formal clothes, but this wasn't a problem. We received a warm and professional welcome, geared towards concrete collaboration. Each faculty has two deans: the departmental dean is Dominican and does not necessarily have a doctorate in the subject, while the academic dean may be a lay person. In Bogotá, the departmental dean of the law faculty is Friar Luis Antonio Alfonso Varas, who has a doctorate in law. We also met the lay dean of the law faculty, Dr Alejandro Gómez Jaramillo.

Initially, we found it difficult to understand their structure because there are several law faculties, one in each city, as well as a distance learning faculty. In each case, there is a division dean and a faculty dean. For theology, classroom teaching in Bogotá differs from distance learning and the professors are not necessarily the same. However, we gradually came to understand, impressed by the professionalism and enthusiastic welcome of the people we spoke to. We discussed a joint master's project in human rights and pedagogy (education sciences), as well as the Unesco Chair project, of course. USTA's law faculty is one of the best in the country, and Colombia is currently experiencing an important milestone for lawyers. In 2016, an agreement was signed between the government and FARC, which was praised worldwide for its rigour and fairness. Nearly five years on, the agreement is due to be evaluated. What has happened to its practical application? The trial is about to begin and the Reconciliation and Truth Commission, chaired by a Jesuit who regularly receives death threats, is doing its work. The balance of this fragile peace is a major issue for Colombia, South America and the world. Lawyers at USTA are involved in this important work, and are in tune with a project such as ours: what about the role of women and religion in post-conflict zones? What about reconstruction and resilience? Which legal processes could contribute to this?

The material and human resources impressed us the most, followed by the enthusiasm and joviality. The welcome was extremely fraternal and open. Furthermore, Lina, the Director of Communications, demonstrated practical qualities that are useful in this kind of meeting, such as outlining possible projects and priorities, in addition to her doctorate in educational science and her perfect English. As the discussions continued, we had lunch together at a nearby restaurant.

Driven by the Director of International Relations, we moved from our 'headquarters' to a nearby district where various departments are located, including the Faculty of Theology. Friar Franklin Buitrago Rojas O.P., whom we have known for a long time and who received us in the training convent, is the dean. We were impressed by the buildings, which appeared to be new to us because, from an European perspective, 10 years is not a significant amount of time for a university building. They are astonished because they see them as old.

The meeting with the lecturers was productive because we were on the same wavelength. Lina and Sister Marie Monnet were both taking notes. The first thing we could organise together would be a Spanish-language master's degree in theology. Accreditation for their own master's degree is expected from the ministry at the end of the month, with a 95% chance of success.

For a bachelor's degree, we thought it would be a good idea to see what's being done in theology at the online teaching faculty. Lina sent me the URL link to find out about it. She also provided me with a link to the university statutes.

In the evening, after walking around the area, we met Friar Fabian Rico, who Adalberto tells me is the only 'rich' person in the community. He is planning to undertake a doctorate in biblical theology. He already has a degree and has spent a significant amount of time at the *Biblicum* in Rome. We spoke to him in French about the École Biblique, classical literature, and contemporary Latin American literature. He recommended some good authors and titles. Marie Monnet put him in touch with Régis Burnet, the vice-dean at the University of Louvain-la-Neuve. Fabian already knew Friar Pierre de Marolles, who was completing his thesis on the Apocalypse at Louvain under the same professor.

The morning is spent exploring the area around the convent and discovering a dreamy little torrent cavorting in a ravine amidst exuberant tropical flora, before heading to the airport, destination Lima! After a turbulent flight, here we are in Peru. In Miraflores, we visited the *Museo de la Memoria*.

The *Museo de la memoria*

In a country of 12 million inhabitants, the civil war from 1980 to 1992 left almost 70,000 people dead and many more wounded and deeply traumatised. The conflict pitted the armed forces against the *Shining Path* and the MRTA, and of course there was fighting between the two rebel groups themselves. Not to mention the 'narcos', who took advantage of the chaos and reaped the rewards.

The museum explores the origins of the conflicts, the brutal nature of terrorism, and the desolation experienced by farming communities, who were often caught in the crossfire. The building is made of rough concrete, generously donated by Germany. The decision to build it was not an easy one, as many people resisted these truths being revealed. The exhibition is educational and, towards the end, offers simple and engaging interactive activities, such as self-expression panels and games for children. As in other countries, such as South Africa after *apartheid*, Rwanda after the genocide and Colombia after the peace agreement with FARC, a Comisión de la Verdad y Reconciliación has been set up. Marie Monnet is particularly interested in restorative justice processes for her Master's degree in Human Rights and for her work with the UNESCO Chair in *Women, Inter-religious Dialogue for Peace and Resilience*.

The next day, we set off for Cuzco, the ancient capital of the Inca Empire, the centre of *Tawantinsuyu, el ombligo del mundo*!

While serving as Director General of the Centro Bartolomé de Las Casas (CBC) until 1997, I realised that the fall of the Berlin Wall and the end of the Shining Path in Peru meant that we could no longer rely entirely on foreign aid. Instead, the beneficiaries would have to contribute to the Centre's resources by developing self-financing. As the Andean College's student residence was not fully occupied, we opened a hotel which was gradually modernised. I supervised the plans for an extension and an additional floor, and I am filled with emotion as I find the room reserved for me for this stay. I marvel at what is now called *Casa de Fray Bartolomé*: a well-equipped, 3-star hotel filled every day with Peruvians who have come with their families for tourism or work. The meeting rooms are still used by all kinds of training groups and for many 'events', as they are called here: meetings of *Medio Ambiente* promoters, for example, like the one happening right now as I write.

The CBC's head office is about a hundred metres away as the crow flies, tucked away in a block of houses to avoid car bombs. A bomb had exploded at the entrance a few months before I arrived in 1992. Miraculously, no one was there at the time, but the door is now armoured. At the entrance, there is a window displaying the *Revista Andina*, a CBC publication and source of pride, founded by Friar Henrique Urbano O.P.

The General Secretary, Yasmin Fernandez G., is waiting for us outside the window of what used to be my office. It is now a large multi-purpose room. Everything has been transformed; partitions have been moved around (if the Incas could make stones walk, why not walls?!) It is such a joy to be here again after twenty-five years!

We meet Valerio Paucarmayta Tacuri, the former General Manager of the CBC and current member of the Management Board responsible for self-financing. We exchange contact details and agree to catch up on Zoom soon. Other CBC employees tell us about their roles. They are often grouped by programme, with three or four employees in each group. They give us a warm welcome. You can sense their commitment and focus.

In the library, we bump into the only person left from 'my time': my colleague Crisaldo Quispe! The library is dedicated to Friar Guy Delran, O.P., from the Dominican Province of Toulouse. He was the founder of the CBC and its director for over 20 years, before my arrival. Throughout the various buildings, the CBC corridors display old photos from the Andean photo library (30,000 glass plates), which have been carefully preserved in acid-free cardboard boxes and catalogued with the help of the American Ford Foundation[167].

We then have an extensive meeting with Cécilia Suerio, the coordinator of the Andean College. She is an anthropologist who conducted her doctoral research in the Puno region, which lies on the border with Bolivia. We discuss the possibilities for collaboration at length. The Andean College offers two postgraduate degrees, one of which focuses on *'Living well, gender and the environment'*. We note that this expression, which is unknown in the academic sphere in Europe, is widely used here in Latin America. This is only the second time it has been used in an academic context. The nature of research here is action-research because it is at the heart of an NGO.

It encourages the participation of those involved in development, invites contributions from grassroots organisations and promotes debate between researchers and practitioners by bringing together different areas of knowledge. According to Cécilia Suerio, this approach involves both decolonial thinking and 'Buen Vivir'. The aim is to *articulate local Andean and Amazonian processes with global epistemological processes.*

Marie Monnet provides more information on *Buen Vivir*, a concept that intrigues us. It originates from the Quechua concept of *sumak kawsay*. This Ecuadorian concept is based on the principle of a harmonious relationship between human beings and nature. It promotes community life based on mutual aid, shared responsibilities and the collective production and distribution of wealth according to each individual's needs. The concept is enshrined in the Bolivian (2009) and Ecuadorian (2008) constitutions.

Cécilia Suerio has agreed to coordinate a collaborative project between Domuni and the Andean College, involving the CBC's

---

[167] See https://cbc.org.pe.

general management. We discussed the possibility of offering one or more joint degrees. Not to mention the Andean College's participation in the Unesco Chair project. Importantly, 'buen vivir' encompasses marginalised or invisible groups, including women, immigrants and the poor.

La Casa Campesina is the CBC's fieldwork programme with *Companeros* –Indian farmers (Quechua, Machiguenga, etc.) who work with the centre in different parts of the country. We then meet Juan de Dios Condori Lope and Ligia Alencastre Medrano. They are both lawyers. We talked at length about the programmes underway at La Casa Campesina. We touched on the issue of community justice and whether it should be integrated into the state justice system. They gave the example of a cattle thief being caught in the act. In this case, the farming community, through its own authorities, would remind the thief of the rules and ask him to make amends. There is no need to call the police! If the same thief reoffends, they are severely punished by the community, who may even execute them. However, since the death penalty is banned by the Peruvian state, the question arises: who is guilty of this crime? Is the person who puts the tyre around the thief's neck and sets it on fire a murderer? Or is he simply carrying out community justice? According to the law, he is a murderer. But if the thief catches pneumonia after being condemned to cross an icy lake at high altitude, who is responsible? These are not just theoretical questions...

We have another intense meeting with Nora Ancassi, a dynamic young professional and intercultural communication specialist. She gives us an excellent presentation on the main project she is responsible for: *Defenders of Human Rights*. The campaign is mainly taking place on social networks and in Lima. Its aim is to support those who speak out against the human and environmental exploitation of mines. In fact, 25 people were murdered the previous month alone for speaking out, and that's just one example of the indifference they face. Nora says she would be interested in working with us, particularly to promote internationally the struggles she and her team are engaged in. These struggles are particularly significant in the areas we want to study.

On Sunday, I was welcomed into my compadre's family. I found my godson, Michel, who has grown up and married Lady. He is now the father of Matthew, who looks exactly like the little Michel I left behind. My godson told me about his job driving for the CBC. He's not based in Cusco, but eight hours away in Apurímac, in the mining area I mentioned above. He told me that he wanted to talk to his coordinator about my wish to collaborate with the CBC. His name was Lino Quintanilla Barbaran. A few days later, I learnt that he had made contact and wanted to speak to me.

The following day, we had a moving meeting with Jean-Jacques Decoster, the Honorary Consul of France in Cusco. We had lived in the city together and crossed paths on several occasions. After I left Cusco, he took up positions at CBC in publishing and then as director of the Andean College. JJD is French, but he studied at American universities. He is an anthropologist and historian specialising in Andean culture, as well as a researcher and professor. He currently teaches at UNSAAC, Cuzco's public university. We discussed the possibility of his working with the Faculty of Social Sciences and mentioned some courses or seminars that he could deliver in French, English and Spanish.

Next, we went to the Dominican convent to meet Friar César Medina, who holds a doctorate in theology from the University of Fribourg. We first met in Lima when he was a professor. A researcher and lecturer in Cuzco, with links to the University of San Martin de Porrés, he has set up a room for lectures, courses and a library just above the Inca Temple of the Sun... and it is in the half-light of a lively night that we evoke the past, dreaming of possible collaborations. Looking out over the cloister, with its various temples spread around it –the temple of the moon, the stars and the sun in this *Koricancha* –we come down a staircase hidden in a small bell tower.

> **The temple of the Sun**
>
> En In Cuzco, the *Koricancha* is the Temple of the Sun, the *'kancha'* or *'place of kori'*, or gold. For five centuries, it has also been a Dominican convent. In one of his Tintin series, The *Temple of the Sun,* Hergé chose to depict this Inca temple in the jungle, with a hidden entrance beneath a waterfall, as this was easier to illustrate. The real Temple of the Sun is virtually intact and located in the city centre. In 1950, an earthquake toppled the colonial walls above it. As with every earthquake, the Inca stones shifted back into place thanks to their concave and convex shapes, which make them resistant to earthquakes. The adobe bricks added during the colonial era have cracked and partly collapsed. They were cleared away along with the plaster that covered them. Today, the stones appear solid and firmly in place: it would be impossible to slip even the slightest piece of paper between them. The elegant colonnades of the cloister frame the different temples: the temple of the moon, the temple of the stars and the temple of the sun. The original straw roof has been replaced by a high metal structure supporting protective Romanesque roof tiles. Architecture emerges in places that are both silent and eloquent. It calls out to a civilisation that has left no written records, like an indelible question in the genes and in the collective unconscious. It was in this exceptional monument that the Las Casas Centre was started as a documentation centre to gather information on the pre-Hispanic past and the colonial period, to study the Quechua language and safeguard oral traditions, in order to mobilise the resources of the past for a reconciled future.
>
> When I was in Cusco, the temple-convent was in a state of severe disrepair. A handful of friars and a few novices lived there, and I sometimes gave Bible classes to the novices. I asked some of them to read the Gospel, but when I realised that they didn't understand what they were seeing, even after going over it several times, I advised them to simply learn how to read. At the end of the agreement that entrusted the Instituto Nacional de Cultura with the management of the historic monument, the prior, Friar Benigno, decided not to renew it, thereby taking over total responsibility for the building and its management. The Instituto Nacional de la Cultura (INC) objected, and it took seven years of litigation for the Dominicans to regain their rights, as Friar Benigno told me when we met again. Now they are entitled to admission tickets, they have set up a marvellous little colonial museum in the church's gallery and a picture gallery in the former refectory, displaying valuable paintings by the Cusquenian school.

After some memorable reunions, the tour of Colombia and Peru came to an end. It heralds great collaborations and a future full of promise.

Argentina, the UNSTA, December 2023

After a 14-hour flight from Paris, we're in top form and off to discover Buenos Aires. 18 km on foot, to start with! We see long avenues, narrow streets, facades in the style of Baron Haussmann and big parks. The Argentinians joke that *it's incredible how Paris has copied Buenos Aires!* It's late spring. The jacarandas are in bloom, competing with the blue of the sky —much like the darker blue of the French flag competing with the lighter blue of the Argentine flag.

We head to the *Immigration Museum*, housed in a huge, well-renovated former hotel that used to welcome migrants when they disembarked from their boats. Inside, visitors can see registers, diplomas (some of which are written in French), black-and-white photographs, and a variety of other objects.

It is a moving experience. Poems and works of art celebrate this geographical and cultural shift. Buenos Aires has the highest number of psychotherapists per square kilometre, even more than New York. Migrants experience a break in their identity, and the following generation looks for its roots.

The next day, we're leaving for San Miguel de Tucumán, which is a two-hour flight away. Although I receive regular emails and WhatsApp messages from our friends at university, I still haven't received an answer to my two questions. We're meeting on Monday, of course, but I'd like to know where and when! I guess I just need to get back into my Latin American habits —everything will work out in its own time!

The aircraft is a Boeing 737 in good condition. The sky is overcast. The border with Uruguay is clearly visible, with large marshes alongside the river and the *Humeda pampas* beyond. One and a half hours after take-off, we land in San Miguel de Tucumán. Argentina is a huge country, five times the size of France. The temperature is 35 degrees.

> **Independence House**
>
> The Declaration of Independence was signed on 9 July 1816 in a simple colonial-style house. The text is written in Spanish, Aymara and Quechua. One of the rooms depicts the battle in which Belgrano's small troop faced off against the royalists (realistas in Spanish —not to be confused with realists): 5,000 against 8,000. At that time, the course of history hinged on a mere handful of men. Coloured spotlights on a model illustrate the movement of the troops, showing that the outcome depended on bold decisions made amid the chaos of battle. I cannot fathom how these small armies could have moved over such long distances with such heavy equipment, including artillery, munitions, camps and provisions, as well as mules and horses.
>
> How could they cross such high passes and cover such long distances without water? The convoy carrying the soldiers' pay arrived in the town as the two armies clashed outside. A group of independence supporters neutralised the convoy, and the news was passed on to Belgrano. The Spaniards retreated by another route, further west, without entering the town. How many thousands of kilometres would they have travelled before returning to Cusco and then Lima? The museum highlights the importance of the women's struggle, in particular that of a mixed-race woman who was promoted to the rank of captain for her determination.

At 9 am, we are on the other side of Independence House, opposite the Dominican convent. The Dominicans played a key role in achieving independence, with two of their members serving as deputies in the Constituent Assembly. The convent has relocated to the left of the church, leaving the colonial wing to the *Universidad del Norte San Tomas de Aquino* (UNSTA) for use as their central headquarters. A modern headquarters has been built in Yerba Buena, the city's upmarket suburb, and it continues to grow. We are warmly welcomed by Luigi Siboni (Dean of the Faculty of Humanities), Victor Martinez (Dean of the Faculty of Economics) and Soledad Paz (Academic Secretary of the Faculty of Humanities). Later, we are joined by Julio, the head of distance learning. His department makes the courses submitted by the faculties available online. Ten per cent of students study online, including all behavioural science students. We all know each other because we have participated in video conferences together. The only person missing is Maximo, who is out of town. On its public website, Domuni presents the joint courses: a

30 ECTS certificate (*diplomatura*), and an MBA in Marketing and Management. We want to develop our collaboration and open it up to other subjects, such as philosophy and theology.

We introduce ourselves and explain the courses and interests of each institution, as well as their situation. Argentina is preparing to adopt the LMD system, also known as the 'Bologna Process', which uses European credits called ECTS. Following the recent election of a new president, Argentina's policy is moving towards radical liberalism and 'joining the market'. This will simplify international transfers. UNSTA is keen to develop distance learning. We then explain the project launched by CIDALC (the coordination body for Dominicans in Latin America and the Caribbean), which aims to organise distance learning courses in Latin America for Latin Americans, with the support of Domuni, the USTA (Dominicans in Colombia), the University of Manizales (Dominican sisters in Colombia), and the UNSTA in Argentina. I explain that we have many contacts and that many lecturers have responded positively. Therefore, we will be able to organise online courses in philosophy, theology and the humanities in 2024. One specific question concerns the organisation of the courses. They can be hosted on UNSTA's Moodle teaching platform, but Domuni would also like to host them on its own platform so that it can organise them and benefit from its 25 years of experience in this area. UNSTA has only been teaching in distance learning mode for two years due to pressure from the covid pandemic. Julio, the educational engineer responsible for distance learning, joined the meeting late. He would prefer the courses to remain on the UNSTA platform, on the grounds that, when a joint activity is proposed, it cannot be organised on both platforms simultaneously. Victor disagreed, pointing out that the decision was not theirs to make and that the Rector would have to be consulted. Julio would like the MBA to be put on hold, with only short, non-degree courses, such as *diplomaturas*, being offered instead. The others protested.

I suggest that, if UNSTA finds itself in a difficult situation, our institution should bear the economic burden of investing in new courses. As Victor points out, there is no need to invest in second-year Master's courses before students have enrolled on the first-year course. Their enrolment fees will cover the cost of subsequent courses. When I suggest that all the courses available in both years should be clearly displayed on the public website, Victor agrees and adds that they could be displayed without first being placed on Moodle. The meeting was productive, with all participants sharing the same experience and interest. At the end of the meeting, Victor took us on a guided tour of the UNSTA headquarters, showing us the amphitheatres, classrooms and ancient cloister. We also met the university's Dominican chaplain. We then set off for Plaza de la Independencia, where the rector joined us at the city's most chic restaurant. The conversation continued. The rector had no problem with the classes being held at the Domuni site, which was a decisive factor for us. We covered a wide range of subjects, from the football World Cup final won by Argentina over France, to opening a bank account in Europe, to domestic politics in France and the "chances" of the far right in the next elections. Naturally, we also sampled some of Argentina's finest wines, which were served alongside delicious local dishes.

The rector, Francesco José López Cruz, took us on a tour of the Yerba Buena site, located some twenty kilometres from the city centre. We discovered a magnificent, modern campus nestled in lush green surroundings, where we met students of medicine and engineering (computer science, etc.). There are laboratories and learning spaces dedicated to care. The campus is very well equipped and functional. Our French universities may well be envious.

Back in the city centre, we were met at the entrance to the convent by Friar Juan José Herrera, OP, who teaches philosophy in various faculties. He offered me an enthusiastic *abrazo*. He completed his doctorate in Toulouse under the supervision of Friar Serge Thomas Bonino, so we had plenty to talk about. He is always willing to take part in training courses. Following these encounters in San Miguel de Tucumán, we moved on to another city.

Córdoba is a huge city on the plains with a population of one and a half million. Apart from a few squares, such as Plaza Colón, it doesn't seem to live up to the guidebooks' portrayal of it as a must-see destination. Despite its historic significance, particularly with regard to its university, Córdoba seems chaotic and rundown. This impression is accentuated by the bad weather; the rain is just the tail end of the terrible storm of the previous days. The pavements are strewn with rubbish and often covered in mud and dirty water, which makes walking difficult. A 'cañada', or vast canalised ditch lined with beautiful trees, runs through the town. This negative impression is dispelled in the evening when the town comes alive. On the banks of the canal, a large bohemian market unfolds, with temporary stalls where second-hand booksellers, art dealers, and craftsmen offer a wide variety of products. People are happy to linger there as musical groups compete with each other: a brass band, an accordion player and dancers. The town has been repopulated. We hurry off to attend Sunday evening Mass in the old Jesuit church. The *Manzana Jesuita* is home to one of the country's first universities and forms the ancient heart of the city. The welcoming church is full of students, and the guitar is played while the preacher calls for trust.

The Dominican Convent is separated from the Dominican Nuns' monastery by a small square, where a discreet plaque marks the location of a mass grave that was used by the military dictatorship in the 1980s. In contrast, the cathedral is made of brown stucco and is not particularly conducive to contemplation.

Our time in Córdoba would have been slightly disappointing if we hadn't visited María José Caram in the afternoon. She lives in a new *barrio*, a *cooperativa de viviendas* (cooperative of homes), 30 minutes from the city centre. On the way, we passed through various neighbourhoods and gained an insight into the poverty experienced by the local population.

I met María José one morning in April 1992 when we landed together on the tarmac at Cusco Airport, ready to embark on a missionary adventure about which we knew nothing. Neither of us knew each other, and the three French friars who were going to support the house in Cuzco –Dominique Motte, Jean-Marc Gayraud and myself– didn't know that a team of three Argentinian sisters, *Las Tucumanas*, had been called to a similar project. One of them was Maria José, who was 30 years old. She was the director of the Andean Pastoral Institute (API) and didn't leave Peru until 2009.

She has a doctorate in theology and is now a full professor at the Jesuit University of Córdoba. It is in this capacity that I have invited her to contribute to the development of our Spanish-language university. Her house is very simple. We don't talk much about the past; it's our new shared project that brings us together. On her computer, she showed us the online courses she was offering. We were amazed at how carefully they were presented, with perfect illustrations. By email, she gave me access to the documents she has published on Academia.edu. She is highly motivated and put us in touch with her network of academics who were ready to collaborate. As the walnut cake was excellent, we lingered for a while.

It was overcast on our return to Buenos Aires. It was time for our final scheduled meetings. Juan Franck welcomed us to the UNSTA headquarters in the capital, where we spent almost two hours discussing the joint training courses we could develop, in Spanish and French. Juan is a true philosopher, and we had the pleasure of discussing the country's trends with him. However, he will be leaving the UNSTA office in Buenos Aires in a month, so it will be difficult for him to work on projects with us. A full *diplomatura* is offered as an online course and corresponds to an introduction to philosophy; it could be offered within the framework of the CIDALC. It is clear that resources are very limited. There are around 150 students across all years and around 30 professors, very few of whom are available due to their low pay. Juan is nervous and stressed. An administrative problem has just arisen that we don't understand: they can no longer receive members of the public in the buildings he showed us, as exams are being held in the convent next to the university. Juan Franck is worried. He understands that we are looking for translators and that our school could hire administrative staff in Argentina, as well as a teacher to provide tutoring. We believe he has an excellent grasp of the administrative requirements of distance learning because he has worked in the Student Reception Department. We are on the same wavelength philosophically and practically. However, we will have to see how institutional issues evolve, including the change of director, rector and academic regent in the Dominican province, not to mention the reforms that the new Argentinian president, Milei, will undertake.

An hour later, we met Sister Cynthia Folquer, the Prioress General of the Dominican Sisters of Tucumán, who is also responsible for history at UNSTA. We had previously met in Cusco, where she had attended the *'Iglesia y realidades socio-económicas'* course organised by the Bartolomé de las Casas Centre. After sharing our memories and analyses, we decided to go to Edelweiss, a historic restaurant in the city, as we couldn't bear to part ways right away. Her father, an agricultural engineer in charge of horticultural research at the University of Tucumán, used to frequent the restaurant whenever he came to the capital for work meetings. Cynthia is a very lively person with bright eyes and a joyful personality. She knows lots of people, has visited Europe and is familiar with the places we come from, including Fanjeaux, Barcelona, Brussels and Rome.

Just as a telephone call or letter can be, the Web is a first step towards a direct meeting. There's no reason to oppose in-person meetings and distance meetings. When the General Secretary of the Bartolomé de Las Casas Centre in Cuzco got married to someone from Canada after exchanging emails, Zoom did not yet exist. We signed a collaboration agreement with UNSTA long before we visited them. Today, our ties have been strengthened by the trip, enabling us to share resources efficiently and trustingly because we already know each other better. So, based on this concrete experience, let's consider the consistency of the network and the interpersonal and interinstitutional relationships that are so important with such a fluid medium as the Web.

An archipiélago of academic institutions

Domuni-Universitas has developed into a network comprising faculty and remote students, and is run by administrative, technical and teaching staff. From 2019 onwards, in response to requests from several isolated universities –including UAC in Congo, UNDH in Haiti, UCM in Madagascar, USDAO in Burkina Faso, Tangaza University in Nigeria, UNSTA in Argentina, and USTA in Colombia –a new type of network was created: a network of universities –a network 'squared': a network of networks. These new links have complemented the collaboration established with European universities, including the University of Lorraine, UCLouvain and ICES. Domuni finds itself at the crossroads between historic universities and those in the process of being established.

The diversity of these establishments means they complement each other, or are 'supplementary', as some would prefer. Imagination is required to fill gaps, adapt processes, combine teaching methods, and integrate different administrative requirements. To reach an agreement, Domuni's managers often have to play both their own part and that of the other party to create a win-win situation. Why is our school particularly well placed to organise collaborations? Because, by offering remote teaching only, it is in direct contact with training centres that also have local roots. Sharing an e-learning course with them is simple.

The idea of a network was there from the very beginning. A name had even been found: UNIDO, almost identical to that of Domuni.

In 2013, an agreement was signed jointly by *La Escuela de Teología en Internet* from Salamanca (Spain), the *Priory Institute* (Ireland) and Domuni (France).

In 2016, eight friars, including several provincials, submitted a petition to the General Chapter in Bologna. They proposed that Dominican universities and training centres be structured into an international network under the name UNIVEROP.

Building on this momentum, the General Curia of the Order established the UNOP-REDOP network in 2022, and its statutes have now been officially approved. Our institution is a member.

But what concrete action has been taken since then? None so far. This is not due to a lack of governance, but rather a lack of leadership.

In such a context, we must take the initiative to give substance to projects that would otherwise remain unrealised.

Domuni has signed bilateral agreements with around thirty centres. Could this bilateral approach be expanded to create a genuine university consortium –a formal alliance between several universities working on joint projects?

The Dominican order in Latin America and the Caribbean, united in the *Conferencia Interprovincial de los Dominicos de América Latina y el Caribe* (CIDALC), have expressed a desire to establish a joint training programme supported by various universities and training centres across the continent.

They called on Domuni through the voice of Friar Jorge Ferdinando Rodriguez Ruiz, OP, Dean of the USTA Distance Learning Faculty. Together with our partners, we are striving to answer this call[168]. In the medium term, we could establish a genuine university consortium.

Globalisation is a fact. Now, we must decide what kind of globalisation we want. By working with the most vulnerable people, our efforts are more likely to succeed. If we pool our resources, we will be able to provide essential services where they are most needed, particularly in research and higher education.

Training a few more theologians in a classroom setting in Rome is not an emergency. Nor is training a few more young people to become traders or speculators.

On the other hand, training theologians in isolated places, working together in Haiti, the DRC, Burkina Faso, Tucumán, to support the creation of small businesses, encouraging inter-religious dialogue and mutual respect in Iraq, Lebanon, Egypt, Pakistan, Africa - these can be at least as useful as multiplying specialist conferences in European capitals.

The quest for excellence, which is often brandished as a watchword, can paralyse or, worse still, blind us to what is really important.[169] But what exactly are we talking about? Is it small circles of mutual admiration? Or ephemeral media recognition?

Excellence is measured by the fruits it yields, not by the ostentatious luxury reserved for a select few researchers or students.

---

[168] *Coming together to provide training for Latin America and the Caribbean, and from Latin America and the Caribbean...*

[169] This concept of excellence is often invoked in university circles to justify elitism and exclusion. However, it should be criticised in light of the Gospel and the Epistles of Saint Paul (Philippians 2; 1 Corinthians 2:1-5; 1 Corinthians 1:26-27). Domuni's mission is characterised by the phrase 'for all'.

Let's focus on original initiatives in the places where humanity is most vulnerable.

A university's objectives must be to promote peace for as many people as possible. They must be based on justice and truth, and therefore on respect for human rights, the duty to remember, and the nurturing of hope and creative solidarity.

The goals of a university network

1. Academic collaboration: Consortium members work together on academic programmes, offering joint or double degrees, as well as research projects and teaching initiatives. This may include organising colloquia and setting up exchange programmes for students and teachers, including internship opportunities.

2. Resource sharing: Partner universities pool resources such as libraries and technology platforms.

3. Joint research: The university consortium promotes collaboration between its member institutions. Such collaboration can lead to larger-scale projects and more significant innovations.

4. Student and faculty mobility: Exchange programmes enabling students and faculty to spend time at partner institutions, thereby fostering greater intercultural understanding and diversifying educational experiences.

5. Development of new programmes: Creating new academic or vocational training programmes to meet emerging labour market and societal needs.

6. Economic benefits: By joining forces, institutions can access greater national and international funding and reduce costs by pooling certain services.

Examples of university consortia include the CIVIS European Civic University, Universitas 21 [170], and the *Agence Universitaire de la Francophonie* (AUF)[171]. These are large, traditional universities with strong national recognition. Our partners are generally much

---

[170] From Belgium to Chile, South Korea to South Africa, our initiatives and programmes [...] are designed to benefit staff, students and member institutions [...] a global network of over 1.2 million students and 250,000 staff. Universitas21 website.....

[171] The AUF - Agence Universitaire de la Francophonie is the world's leading university network, with more than 1,000 universities and scientific research centres in nearly 120 countries. Created in 1961. AUF website .....

more heterogeneous. The African Virtual University (AVU)[172] model is therefore a good reference.

To gain a clearer understanding of the integration model, let's spend a moment reflecting on the idea of networks, the archipelago metaphor, and the concept of communion.

Before I left for Peru, I wrote a short pamphlet containing mystical observations bearing the paradoxical title: *Islands on Terra Firma*. This redundancy emphasised the soundness of the apophthegms that formed strong anchor points in my contemplation as a long-distance sailor, poet, and wandering mystic. The title wasn't mine; it belonged to a 16th century document which referred to Mexico as 'terra firma' and the great Caribbean islands as *las islas de la tierra firme* –the islands of the mainland. A new world, hitherto unknown, was looming on the horizon like a dark, bluish mass. It was emerging as an essential partner for an old world in need of rethinking.

To gain a clearer understanding of the integration model, let's spend a moment reflecting on the idea of networks, the archipelago metaphor, and the concept of communion.

Before I left for Peru, I wrote a short pamphlet containing mystical observations bearing the paradoxical title: *Islands on Terra Firma*. This redundancy emphasised the soundness of the apophthegms that formed strong anchor points in my contemplation as a long-distance sailor, poet, and wandering mystic. The title wasn't mine; it belonged to a 16th century document which referred to Mexico as 'terra firma' and the great Caribbean islands as *las islas de la tierra firme* –the islands of the mainland. A new world, hitherto

---

[172] The African virtual university streams its courses via satellite [...] In four years, this institution has enrolled more than 24,000 students, streamed some 3,500 hours of courses and set up 26 education centres in 16 countries across the continent. The experiment has worked better in English-speaking African countries [...] because governments and populations have better integrated this method of training, whereas French-speaking African countries do not recognise diplomas awarded by distance learning. Sophie Condat, 'L'université virtuelle africaine', Revue internationale d'éducation de Sèvres, 31 December 2002, online since 24 November 2011. DOI : https://doi.org/10.4000/ries.1806 Top of page.

unknown, was looming on the horizon like a dark, bluish mass. It was emerging as an essential partner for an old world in need of rethinking.

> **Meditation XVII (1624), John Donne**
>
> *No man is an island,*
> *Entire of itself,*
> *Every man is a piece of the continent,*
> *A part of the main.*
> *If a clod be washed away by the sea,*
> *Europe is the less.*
> *As well as if a promontory were.*
> *As well as if a manor of thy friend's*
> *Or of thine own were:*
> *Any man's death diminishes me,*
> *Because I am involved in mankind,*
> *And therefore never send to know for whom the bell tolls;*
> *It tolls for thee*

The poem is less about an archipelago than a jigsaw puzzle. It quickly moves on to the image of the *tierra firme*, where each person is just *a piece of the continent,* a mere part of the whole.

If the first evocation rings true, the following, in contrast, resonates strangely: it becomes stifling, even totalitarian.

Every man... a part of the whole. But then, where is the subject? The hypostasis? The person? Is it the continent that speaks, or the little plots of land? Who says 'I'? The human species, or each of us personally? The puzzle, or its scattered pieces?[173]

Another question arises: do my boundaries strictly follow those of my neighbours? Do I have to adjust to the pieces around me? It soon becomes clear that the two metaphors –that of the island and

---

[173] I once knew a genetics professor who liked to say that organisms are a trick of genes to reproduce themselves. Therefore, the fundamental subject would be the gene, rather than the human individual. Conversely, some philosophers favour the human species over the individual. Some Eastern mystics invoke the Great Whole, in which the illusion of individuality dissolves and the atman merges with Brahman.

that of the pieces of a jigsaw puzzle –are incompatible. An island is not a piece of a jigsaw puzzle. It has its own outline and, above all, an empty, free maritime space with no fixed shape. An island is a complete entity, and on the horizon we can see other 'wholes', both similar and different, which do not touch because if two islands touch, they merge into one. So, while Santo Domingo and Haiti are two countries, they are also one island –the *two wings of the same dove*, as President Aristide poetically put it, in an attempt to transfigure the often cruel opposition between the two.

The archipelago metaphor is transformed in unexpected ways as we ascend to higher altitudes. The Andes are characterised by isolated valleys, with glaciers upstream and impassable ravines downstream acting as natural barriers.

On the Peruvian coast, impenetrable deserts separate them.

Before the advent of motors, you had to navigate your way from one valley to the next, either by climbing up streams to the top and then descending into the next valley, or by following the streams themselves. This was a long journey, but there were springs along the way. This fragmentation has led to the emergence of independent contemporary civilisations that are isolated and protected by the arid desert and the distance that separates them.

When moving from America to Africa, one's imagination turns to oases linked by camel caravans. Rather than being isolated islands, these are rare wells that dot the desert landscape.

Transposing the image into the realm of linguistics, we encounter the Tower of Babel. Rather than being a punishment, the division of languages is a liberation from the 'whole', or the singular (the singular thought of a wooden language or a language of figures that do not need to be translated). It confers independence, allowing each community to flourish and develop its own unique culture. This process of individualisation certainly calls for overcoming.

No man is an island, in the sense that we need to communicate, exchange and trade with others to develop our sense of self. We must be able to share goods, as well as the signs that designate them. We must visit each other to get to know one another, practise hospitality, form alliances, get married...

In the Order of Preachers, we speak of a province as a communion of convents. And the Order is made up, internationally, of a communion of provinces. A network of networks, a communion of communions, therefore, invisible, like 'the communion of saints'?

The archipelago theme resonates with me. Each island - much like each training centre, whether large or small - can maintain its own identity while working together. This reflects the culture of the European Union: *unity in diversity*.

Afterword

*If the fire burnt down my house, what would I take with me?
I'd like to take the fire with me...*[174]

From Domuni, I will cherish the intensity of life - its renewal and unpredictability - around two words: transmission and otherness.

The alterity of techniques, which are constantly evolving... The alterity of staff, in all their diversity and uniqueness: students, faculty, administrative staff... The alterity of institutions... The alterity of disciplines, languages, cultures, religions...

Yes: alterity and transmission. After all, life is all about dialogue, reciprocity, listening and passing things on. All of Domuni's efforts are organised around this transmission of experience, knowledge, research and questions, in a tradition that rejoices in new beginnings.

I will always remember Domuni as an invisible, timeless communion that is paradoxical and sensitive, and which offers a foretaste of the communion of saints. Some of the people involved in its first twenty-five years have passed away. There is no need to engrave a list: they have not been forgotten. Until that eternal summer that will bring us all together, we continue to communicate, again and again. Until that final moment[175], this celebration will be full of true brotherhood and sisterhood, and no one will be excluded.

I believe in it and hope for it: victorious love transcends all forms of distance, both spatial and temporal, and establishes a living communion that never ceases to surprise us. I can already sense this on the teaching platform.

---

[174] Jean Cocteau, *Clair-obscur*, 1954.
[175] Ep: 1,10.

To our reader friend

Dear reader, thank you for still being here. This book was intended to be more of a conversation than a traditional story – you may have noticed the liberal use of exclamation marks! Rather than following the chronological order of a story, I followed the sequence of ideas, answering your questions as I went along. You could hear the rumour of a thousand trickles from the spring. You listened to the roar of stones laden by the torrent. You have rested on the plain at the peaceful confluence of the streams. You worried about our identity as we made our way to the ocean.

My final point is a question mark. It is up to others, perhaps you, to write the rest.

The future is invisible, yet it is right in front of us. In my introduction, I suggested looking back at the road travelled and sharing the photo taken by smartphone with friends. However, the future cannot be photographed. We can only guess at it and hope for it.

Behold, I am making a new world,
that is already coming to life: don't you see it?[176]

---

[176] Es: 43,19.

Appendices

Appendix 1:
The Internet and Christian learning

In January 2017, Sister Marie Monnet was invited to the *Maison de la Conférence Épiscopale de France* on Avenue de Breteuil to give a presentation to French diocesan educators on 'Internet and Christian learning'. She called for the creation of a global inter-diocesan training programme backed up by personalised local support. The idea was clear, simple and achievable, but unfortunately it didn't gain any traction. Dioceses have no experience of working together, which is why Domuni needs to develop gradually.

Here is the transcript of her address:

What already exists:

I spent a few days with my family over the All Saints' Day holiday. My nephews are aged between six and eleven. I helped them with their homework. Children in primary school and Year 7 at secondary school work on digital tablets. This is today's pupils' new schoolbag. The textbook is online and is updated regularly by the teachers. Pupils can use it to prepare homework and parents can use it to access termly reports and information about attendance.

Pupils have access to all the resources they need, including poetry for learning purposes, maps for studying, English videos, music for listening to and geometry exercises. These resources include written content, 3D diagrams, photos, short videos and audio files, such as interviews with pen pals from Germany or Italy.

The tablet facilitates interactive engagement, encouraging children to actively participate in the digital environment rather than remaining passive.

Teaching methods have changed dramatically in just a few years, so it's only natural for a 10-year-old to type a keyword into Google to find out more about a country or painting. This is their first instinct when preparing a presentation. The internet is now the main source of knowledge. Pupils have a wealth of information at their fingertips, so the teacher's role is to gradually help them learn how to prioritise, analyse and present information.

My nephews are not enrolled at a school in San Francisco or Dubai. They attend a small, private, Catholic, family-run school in Saint-Gervais-les-Bains in the Chamonix Valley, which is run by the *Sœurs de l'Assomption*. It was there that I became aware of the profound and rapid transformation taking place in the world of education. In less than 10 years, all "adults" will have received this kind of training.

Here is another significant example. My youngest cousin is in the final year of her medical degree and has already started her internship. For the last seven years, she has received all her lessons online and studied them at home every morning. At 1 pm, she goes to the hospital to learn how to practise medicine. From now on, we will be receiving treatment from young doctors who have never attended a traditional in-person course.

Over the last twelve years or so, e-learning has become the preferred method of professional development. A former IBM executive pointed this out to me straight away during the break.

Today, the Church is connected. Parishes and dioceses all have their own websites. The internet undoubtedly creates links and brings new life. The weekly bulletin, readings for the following Sunday, biblical commentaries, resources and conferences can all be accessed online. These can be read or listened to via audio replay, as can songs from the liturgy and sheet music for musicians. Universal prayer and all services (sick visits, sacraments, reception services and social services) are also easily accessible. You can even take part in online retreats such as Retraite dans la Ville or Marche dans la Bible, which are hosted by the Dominicans in Lille and attract over 50,000 participants[177]. I preached there in 2016. Each biblical commentary sparks other comments from readers who then interact with each other, sharing thoughts and sometimes even challenging each other. It is not unusual for more than 100 comments to be exchanged daily by Christians from all over the world who have two things in common: their faith and their language.

I recently visited the Holy Land with a group of young professionals. Before we left, we created a WhatsApp group for the different members, which enabled us to communicate freely throughout our stay. We could comment, exchange messages and joke around (even though we were in different vehicles). There was face-to-face dialogue, as well as a second, parallel dialogue on WhatsApp. Today, several months after we returned, we are still using the group to talk to each other. We can share a press article about Israel or Palestine, something we have read, or our feelings about an event in the Middle East. It's a simple way to stay in touch and keep the spirit of the trip alive. It's a modern medium that appeals to the younger generation because they are comfortable using it and engage with it enthusiastically. These media evolve all the time: after blogs came Facebook, Twitter, YouTube, WhatsApp, Snapchat and Instagram, to name a few. The challenge is to engage with the younger generations, and it's clear that the internet is their continent, where they feel at home.

I recently visited the Holy Land with a group of young professionals. Before we left, we created a WhatsApp group for the different members, which enabled us to communicate freely throughout our stay. We could comment, exchange messages and joke around (even though we were in different vehicles). There was face-to-face dialogue, as well as a second, parallel dialogue on WhatsApp. Today, several months after we returned, we are still using the group to talk to each other. We can share a press article about Israel or Palestine, something we have read, or our feelings about an event in the Middle East. It's a simple way to stay in touch

---

[177] In 2024, the figure is 150,000 enrolments.

and keep the spirit of the trip alive. It's a modern medium that appeals to the younger generation because they are comfortable using it and engage with it enthusiastically. These media evolve all the time: after blogs came Facebook, Twitter, YouTube, WhatsApp, Snapchat and Instagram, to name a few. The challenge is to engage with the younger generations, and it's clear that the internet is their continent, where they feel at home.

In a few years' time, all Christians, regardless of generation, will be living in a fully connected world. If we project forward five years, Christian education will necessarily have to take place online (at least in part), using digital tools, in order to reach the generations of Christians of formative age. They will need to understand and master this new pedagogy, which is already being used in schools, universities and businesses. Teachers' roles are changing, not because they are becoming less important, but because they need to adapt to new ways of transmitting knowledge. This may seem obvious, but it's important to be aware of it because not everyone shares this view. The internet is still sometimes contested, as if we had a choice. Not only do we not have a choice, but we can also be pioneers and pathfinders who give the internet a soul. As educators and Christians, we can take responsibility for inhabiting this new continent and enchanting this new world.

Therefore, Christian education needs to be rethought to take the digital factor into account. Digital technology can also benefit Christian education.

In what ways can the internet serve the lives and education of Christians? The question is not about replacing existing methods, but about using a new form of communication.

- The internet is part of everyday life. While it doesn't replace meetings, it can prepare for them. It enables people who are unable to travel to still be involved, as well as providing other means of communication. In that sense, it's an alternative. I sometimes hear people express concern that the internet will replace what exists in person. However, the reality is that with the internet, we can reach people who would not be able to travel anyway.

- Answer questions, structure content, encourage students and help them overcome technical or psychological difficulties. Create a sense of community and collective enthusiasm through meditation and contemplation. This is because what we study is not disconnected from spiritual life; on the contrary, it leads to admiration, praise and prayer. Multimedia is the medium for a new pedagogy that needs to be developed.

Ideally, there should be comprehensive training across the diocese, followed by personalised support in the local communities, with better-trained people to help learners.

- Of course, there's the content, but the way it's communicated also plays a big part. While the content of the faith may be the same, the way it is presented is also very important. It is just like the way a product is packaged. This is important for its transmission and reception. It is not the same as presenting younger generations with parchments written in an ancient script that we no longer know how to decipher, even if the illuminations are beautiful! Just as there was a time for illumination, there is now a time for the internet.

Focus on online Christian training:

Complete degree courses are available online. While I mentioned this in relation to medicine, the same applies to law, the human and social sciences, history, philosophy, and theology. You can follow complete university courses leading to bachelor's and master's degrees in theology entirely by distance learning. Simply search for *'distance learning theology'* or *'distance learning licence in theology'* online. Certain keywords will bring up a list of courses on offer. You can then submit your application online. Once your enrolment has been validated, you will be connected to a distance learning platform.

These courses require a high level of basic knowledge, as well as time, patience, and good organisational skills. A great deal of autonomy is essential in order to cope with the solitude of intellectual work, which is even more important online. Study is the main asceticism in the Order of Preachers to which I belong. To support you, meetings are organised and online tutoring is available, so you know there are people behind the screens! Gradually, a study community forms, which is particularly enriching because you meet people you would never have encountered in your immediate circle.

After studying the courses, completing the homework and passing the exams, the student graduates. That's what happens for a university degree. This is the top of the pyramid.

Short, targeted courses are also available. For those with less time to spare, there are shorter learning formats and more intensive modes of study, such as certificates and university diplomas. These courses can be taken alone or in a group. We have extensive experience of groups of Christians from different regions who come together around a person or community, such as the Lay Dominicans in Nantes, or parish groups, such as the Rangueil parish in Toulouse and the Chant d'oiseau parish in Brussels. Eight to ten people take the same course or unit and work on it together. Each person receives the entire course, which is broken down into sections. Each person reads a section, and then the group meets to discuss it once a fortnight or once a month. A facilitator, perhaps a theologian or someone with more training, helps the group to understand better, put questions into perspective, overcome possible misunderstandings, and go further.

The advantage is that, wherever they are, people can access solid content when a local specialist is not always available. This is the principle of sharing that the internet makes possible. The law faculties in France have joined forces to create a digital university, where the best professors deliver courses and every student has access to them, regardless of their location. For example, you can take a course at Harvard, as some of its renowned professors have made their courses available online to make them accessible to everyone, not just those who can afford prestigious education. This is how the "democratisation" of higher education via the internet is achieved. To put it another way, the term means **making the richness of the Christian tradition available to all**.

'*A la carte*' courses can address a specific concern or provide a particular skill. Anyone who wants to read about a subject in depth can take each course. For instance, a doctor might choose an ethics course, a catechist might choose a Bible course and a secondary school teacher might choose a history course. Free, open-access resources can be found on Google, where keywords can be used to explore subjects in greater depth. On the Domuni website, we have chosen to make these resources more accessible by classifying them by video, audio, text, homily, and so on. The teaching team selects and organises these resources to ensure they are of a high quality, to guide learners and to save them time. There are many online resources to choose from, which complement what is available in bookshops and training centres.

The aim of this first part was to assess what is available, and to recognise the richness and diversity of the resources and content on offer. The internet is not replacing face-to-face training centres, as is often feared, but it is opening up new possibilities: a new audience, a new way of learning and accessing knowledge, and a new dialogue with contemporary culture. We have the means to contribute to a 'soul supplement' –a way of being on the internet that humanises it and breathes new life into it –and this is an opportunity for us, at the heart of the Church. In short, the internet is a means of forming Christians, and Christians can use it evangelically. We are gathered here to improve access to Christian training and culture and to promote an understanding of the faith that is both *intellectual* and *heartfelt*–a theological faith that is practised, prayed for and shared.

What can we imagine?

Digital communion is possible. Each diocese has the means, limited and insufficient, to make a global offer of what we can dream of, from the point of view of media, content, attractiveness, pedagogy, advertising and administration.

Nor is there a 'market' –a number of people who are potentially interested –that would justify such an investment for a diocese or apostolic region. Could a think tank be created to consider and identify what is appropriate in terms of target audience, needs, expectations and weaknesses? Could all existing resources in terms of content, such as written documents, videos and audio, be pooled? What about an inter-diocesan distance learning course open to the French-speaking world? I'm thinking of countries such as those in

Africa, Madagascar and Mauritius. This could involve training that links with what is happening in the dioceses and establishes a 'digital communion', including meetings, summer universities and Bible sessions.

Ideally, the course would be certified by the Church of France. It could be designed as a highly flexible pathway. The important thing is to start the process. Not just one path. Not one more obligation. It shouldn't be about obtaining a diploma at all costs. Couldn't we envision a training booklet certified by the Church of France that would be completed throughout one's life? It could be adapted to the individual's circumstances, interests, and stages of life. Today, we think less in terms of a 'one-size-fits-all' approach to shaping someone and more in existential terms. Training is there to give meaning, to stimulate curiosity, and to provide depth.

It would be useful to provide training that gives people a sense of responsibility. Christian education is about more than just the transfer of knowledge or the acquisition of a diploma. It is about cultivating your talents throughout your life. From the trainer's perspective, this requires humility, modesty, and trust in others. For the Dominicans, students are primarily responsible for their own education. The role is not to take charge of children or a flock, but to act as an interlocutor, guide, adviser and pathfinder.

Our students are doctors, lawyers, craftsmen, fathers and mothers, capable men and women. They are responsible in the truest sense of the word and accountable for their faith. This ability must be developed and honed. That's the whole point of the apprenticeship. The ability to speak, respond and give your opinion requires an intellectual journey: training and a progressive structuring of the faith. Our students are short on time and certainly don't want to go backwards. So, how can our Christian training courses gradually enable them to speak about what is essential –about God –in a way that is relevant in today's world?

APPENDICES

Can the internet phenomenon be interpreted theologically?

Saint Paul speaks of a recapitulation. Ephesians 1:9-10: *9 making known to us the mystery of his will, according to his purpose, which he set forth in Christ 10 as a plan for the fullness of time, to unite all things in him, things in heaven and things on earth.* (ESV)

The recapitulation of knowledge and the density of communication are in harmony with Saint Paul's vision of the **fulfilment** of the universe and history. This **analogy** is one of the **signs** of the times and allows us to understand what is happening on a deeper level.

Working with and through the internet requires a deep conviction that everyone has something to say. There is a fundamental trust in human intelligence and a deep trust in humanity that is desired by God. This positive outlook should be cultivated to the point of giving people a voice and making them interlocutors, not just receivers.

We need to consider the internet through the lens of the Trinitarian structure of gift. There is a **research community** that connects us: the only way we can connect with each other so closely while respecting one another, without destroying, consuming or plagiarising each other, is through love. This relationship of love and friendship in diversity is the essence of God's life, who is both one and three. It is about living God and living the love that is God. God is not an old man bored on a cloud; creation is called upon to join this **dance** of communication, collective thought and the resurrection of the past.

The Internet phenomenon is a breath of fresh air, a Spirit. The internet is a tool that favours **synthesis, exchange, solidarity** and **creativity**. However, it also seems threatening because it brings us together and brings us so close that our identities are vulnerable to damage.

What model represents this unity and diversity? Where is this communication most evident? Where is this mutual recognition achieved? If not in the God in whom we believe –three in one, mutual love –then where is this **relationship that is constitutive** of the other?

Appendix 2: The 20th anniversary
Thomas Aquinas and Domuni Universitas

Do you know how many words are attributed to Saint Thomas? He is said to have written nearly nine million words in 22 years, which equates to an average of more than 1,000 words a day. This leads me to believe that he would have appreciated the internet.

Firstly, for its speed, because Thomas was in a hurry. His thoughts went much faster than his hands, and he began to use a mode of writing so simplified and full of abbreviations that it was described as unintelligible. Somewhere between a text message and a Tweet!

Secondly, Thomas would have loved the teamwork that the internet requires.

It has been said that he dictated to secretaries, that he could tire out three of them in a day and that he even dictated to three secretaries at once. Even worse, it is said that he dictated in his sleep! Should we not be talking about assistants and associates who were capable of thinking and writing, like the man who finished the *Summa Theologica*? Isn't this what we would call a collective intelligence enterprise today, thanks to the internet?

We can picture Saint Thomas's writing study as a painter's studio, perhaps like those of Rembrandt or Rubens. They would provide their assistants with the main instructions, oversee the work, and reserve the drawing of faces and hands for themselves. In St Thomas's works, you can see the passages he wrote himself in his hurried, *illegible* handwriting.

It was during Thomas's time that tables of contents and indexes were invented, and the quest for vast knowledge became a passion. People would consult several books at once and read a lot, but not necessarily everything. Thomas would have loved to have had almost immediate access to the world's libraries at the click of a mouse! He would have loved the Gallica digital library and the extensive digitisation of sources.

The choice of this patronage for the inauguration of our portal is a logical one. Through Saint Thomas, Domuni has inherited a taste for innovation, a desire to synthesise knowledge, and a passion for communicating it. Domuni has also inherited Thomas's way of thinking, believing and bearing witness.

1° A way of thinking that can be characterised by the harmonious reconciliation of what is often artificially opposed: soul and body, form and content, contemplative life and active life, intelligence and faith, message and medium.

2° A way of believing, that is, of having confidence, confidence to tackle the digital continent, to cross linguistic borders, to move mountains, to find resources for projects, to commit with magnanimity, to trust others to create vast networks together.

3° A way of bearing witness, of demonstrating that the message is not exclusive, that it belongs to everyone, and that it is our responsibility to make it accessible and clear, while ensuring that it is of high quality.

Let us pray to God with Saint Thomas, asking Him to enable us to enter ever more deeply into the joyful impulse of His communication.

Brother Michel Van Aerde

Appendix 3:
Digital learning centres in the interfaith debate

Conference in Erbil (Kurdistan) in 2022, speech by Michel Van Aerde in English. The subject I am about to address is very close to my heart. It concerns the role of digital learning centres in inter-religious dialogue.

For me, this is more than just a theoretical question. I firmly believe that this is a project that needs to be carried out and deserves real effort. The difficulties are not financial or technical, but rather have to do with having an open mind and heart. Let's meet again in a few years to see if we have made any progress. My starting point is an observation and a reminder of the dangers of internet communication. While it facilitates contact, it also increases the risk of conflict. However, these exchanges also provide tremendous opportunities for mutual understanding, dialogue and, if possible, friendship.

Building on this observation, I would like to present an outline for an inter-university project. This project would take a realistic approach, proposing three levels or steps for inter-institutional exchange within a network.

Finally, in the third part, I will propose ways to restore the role of intellectuals in the city. Universities play a vital role in countering extreme, biased and partisan views. In order to combat fake news, we require an impartial intellectual authority. It is within universities that the search for truth based on scientific criteria is taking place. This effort should be intensified by strengthening university networks and ensuring the dissemination of results.

There are therefore three parts:

(1) A report and analysis of the state of religious -related communication on the Internet.

(2) A project to set up an inter-university training and research network.

(3) Strengthening the influence of academic intellectuals on public opinion in order to counter fake news and propaganda.

The aim is to progress from a chaotic juxtaposition of partial information on religions to organised training courses and integrated practical and theoretical research between universities.

The internet can be used to spread violent messages. However, it can also facilitate dialogue and the sharing of wisdom. As we know, genuine mutual understanding between religions can help to dispel prejudice and aggression. It enables people to meet and exchange ideas. Through dialogue, each religion can discover its own unique characteristics, and rather than leading to syncretism, this openness can strengthen the best aspects of each identity.

The internet makes a great deal of knowledge accessible. However, there is an enormous amount of information available in a haphazard way across a wide variety of sites. This information can be accessed by entering keywords into search engines. There are also coherent training courses organised by institutions, particularly universities. If the aim is to increase capacity and accessibility, the internet is the ideal tool.

Digital universities can facilitate the transition from confrontation to dialogue. It is crucial to encourage faculty members, students and researchers to interact with each other on shared platforms. These platforms enable people to travel without leaving their homes. They enable everyone to experience the richness of a place, culture or religion while respecting the privacy of others. They offer the challenge of being two or many while remaining oneself. How do they achieve this? They maintain distance through the platform while enabling sharing. In this sense, the distance introduced by the internet enables relationships. The proximity made possible by the internet also enables a form of communion. In religious education, everyone has the opportunity to delve deeper into their own religion and achieve excellence at bachelor's, master's and doctoral levels.

Three levels of accreditation and inter-university collaboration:

The first step for a university is to offer courses on each religion, which could be taught by people belonging to the majority religion at that university. This already exists at Domuni Universitas, for example.

The second step could be to invite teachers of the religion being taught: a Hindu would teach Hinduism, a Buddhist would teach Buddhism, a Jew would teach Judaism, a Christian would teach Christianity, a Muslim would teach Islam, a Vodouist would teach Vodou, and so on. This approach is simple, but does not yet exist.

The third step could be inter-university cooperation, involving not only universities of the same religion, but also cross-disciplinary, inter-confessional collaboration for joint programmes. This could be achieved by forming a consortium of universities and would greatly benefit peace.

Universities have a role to play in distinguishing between what is rigorously established and what is mere manipulation. This involves giving scholars full authority and restoring academic authority in public opinion. As in Socrates' time, philosophers stand up to those who talk nonsense, sometimes risking their lives for the truth. Throughout history, many have paid this price. Their role is essential in society.

Where points of debate arise, impartial juries can help to ensure rigorous discussion. The Dominicans experienced this during the period of Catharism, prior to the Crusades. We need to revive the medieval tradition of *disputatio*. To achieve this, university debates must move away from the confidentiality of overly specialised colloquia, get out of the laboratories and tackle pressing issues. They must also be widely disseminated through books, magazines and blogs. Academic rigour must be made accessible through the media.

Difficult situations are always resolved by the commitment of active minorities. The important thing is the quality of the movement initiated, which then spreads naturally. Even if there aren't many of us, let's start at our own level and find a way to exchange ideas on what's essential: things that can give meaning and structure to personalities, encourage generosity and set an example. The internet offers us a unique tool for meeting, sharing, and disseminating information.

Appendix 4:
A noospheric adventure

Revue *Noosphère*, September 2021, n° 15, Extensive interview, with Brother Michel Van Aerde.

The editorial committee chose to interview Dominican friar Michel Van Aerde about the adventure of Domuni, the online university of which he is currently rector after having founded it 22 years ago.

<u>The Editorial Board</u>: *You are the rector of an original and very avant-garde university: international, multilingual, distance learning... When you launched it 22 years ago, you were a pioneer! A sort of "noospheric" adventure! Can you explain to our readers both its origins and its meteoric rise?*

<u>Brother Michel Van Aerde</u>: "At the outset, 22 years ago, Domuni was just a dream. It was a vision that carried it through, turning the dream into reality.

When Domuni began, Timothy Radcliffe was Master of the Dominican Order. He encouraged people to dream with him, saying, "Let's dream together". The process of imagining and dreaming positively is fascinating. It's a form of faith. Just like Joseph, the man of dreams in the Bible. Domuni was indeed a dream at first, almost a form of play. Then it became a start-up.

Having just been elected Provincial of Toulouse, I discovered that although there were significant demographic resources in the form of well-trained young friars, this would not be enough to meet the needs of the world, especially in faraway places. Together, we dreamed and started writing projects. The first step towards realising these projects was taken by Friar Hervé Ponsot, who had studied at HEC.

The Domuni Association was founded in 1999 by two French Dominican provinces. The first website was built and the first employee hired.

DOMUNI, A COLLECTIVE ADVENTURE

The Dominican province of Toulouse and the province of France (the name is a legacy from the Middle Ages) have traditionally been mutually stimulating. The idea of bringing the two provincial councils together in the same place to decide on the creation of an association and implement a project that did not yet exist seemed totally impossible. And yet it happened! Everyone voted separately to form a joint association. We told ourselves, 'There will only be a real institution if we work together; otherwise, we'll fall into a system of co-optation. Since we are in competition with each other, we are going to be demanding about how the institution works'. And so it was. This dream came true slowly and in secret because what was happening online was not visible to everyone.

What exactly were Domuni's objectives when you created it?

The idea was to use the internet to reach students who lived far from university centres. I had just spent five years in Cusco, Peru, at an altitude of 3,400 metres (Friar Michel Van Aerde was running a research and action NGO called the Bartolomé de Las Casas Centre in a context of great poverty following the Sendero Luminoso civil war. The internet, still in its infancy, provided a link to the most developed centres of study and communication.)

The idea for Domuni Universitas originated from the perspective of Latin American theology: Domuni was conceived with the poorest in mind. Thanks to the internet, Dominican teaching, which had previously been accessible only to a select few, could now be accessed by anyone, anywhere in the world. The Dominican tradition is based on transmission and exchange. Its encounter with technology based on horizontal exchange was therefore inevitable.

This initiative has its roots in the Dominican Order, which is no small matter. Can you tell us more about how Domuni is rooted in this intellectual tradition, organisational structure and teaching mission?

The Dominicans are not a homogeneous group; no human group is. They trace their roots back to the democratic movement of the 13th century. They were founded in Toulouse, where there were capitouls; at the time, in the cities, the bourgeoisie organised themselves democratically against the nobility. Dominique[178] also sent his disciples to university, where there were still very few students and one of the professors was English.

Firstly, democracy; secondly, the university; and thirdly, the international dimension: three fundamental and structuring points. This represents a break with feudalism and the patriarchal Benedictine organisational model. With the Dominicans, democracy permeates every level of the organisation. They are the only order in Catholicism where the master is not confirmed by the Pope. Underpinning this model is the implicit theology that the Spirit does not come from above, but is among us on the ground. This is the gospel of fraternity, which must be lived in order to bear witness to it. Every baptised person has received the Spirit and does not need a superior to take charge of them; the prior is not a superior, but rather is a friar who animates.

The prior replaces the father abbot of the Benedictine model; he is not elected for life, only for a limited time and with counter-powers, the councillors and the conventual chapter. It is democracy in action. This experience has helped us to think differently. For example, Friar Francisco de Vitoria[179], in Spain, can be considered the founder of international law; he taught in Salamanca (a room bears his name at the UN). Evangelically organised fraternal life therefore has a particular dynamism of which we are not necessarily aware at the beginning; it takes time to discover this heritage.

When Domuni was launched, our students trusted us. Everything depends on trust. They trusted the Dominicans to teach theology. It was almost as if all of Domuni's lecturers were Thomas Aquinas, or closer to home, Marie-Dominique Chenu or Yves Congar. It was as if all the biblical scholars had founded the École Biblique de Jérusalem and all the legal scholars were Francisco Vitoria or Bartolomé de las Casas, the founder of human rights.

In fact, when we are online, we are somewhat removed from physical space and time. We are all concentrated in the same place

---

[178] Dominic de Guzman, founder of the Dominicans (c. 1170-1221).

[179] Francisco de Vitoria, Dominican theologian and jurist of the School of Salamanca (c. 1480-1546).

and all contemporaries. Tradition is close at hand, as are great individuals. It's an intellectual communion of saints. Saint Paul said that everything would be 'summed up' in Christ, 'anaképhalésastai', concentrated and gathered together. It's like an anticipated experience.

As I said, the decentralised democratic structure of the Dominican Order, the Order of Preachers, has served it well for eight centuries and makes it particularly suited to the internet. It is a network of communities, study centres, sisters, lay people, brothers and friends. It transcends borders, languages and sensitivities. All of this has been gradually mobilised to provide Domuni with a wealth of high-quality teaching resources.

Domuni received immediate encouragement from the General Chapters, which take place every three years, and support from successive Masters of the Order. This began with Timothy Radcliffe, who blessed the project's inception. This was then continued by Carlos Aspiroz and finally by Bruno Cadoré, who was President of Domuni at the time of his election.

The president of Domuni today is Friar Jean-Jacques Pérennès, who is the director of the École Biblique et Archéologique Française in Jerusalem. Friar Guido Vergauwen was rector of the University of Fribourg in Switzerland for a decade. Domuni is a network rooted throughout the Dominican Order. Friars and sisters teach on every continent, including India, Africa, Australia, North and South America, and, of course, Europe and the Middle East, as we teach in French, English, Spanish, Italian and Arabic.

Then we made that dream a reality. It was completely innovative in 1999, when the French were just discovering the internet after the Minitel... We were on our own. Some people thought it was impossible. Fortunately, the first students believed in it. This was particularly the case because it was theology, and in France, theology doesn't lead to a job; it's a luxury that you pursue out of passion, without worrying about the diploma, grades or exams. As the number of students grew, so did the number of lecturers, and we were able to set up a master's degree, and then several more, as well as the courses needed to create a licence in theology. The amount of voluntary work was considerable. It still is. The students and professors are motivated, and that produces quality. The studies are modestly priced and there is a bursary system to ensure that financial constraints do not prevent anyone from studying.

You referred to Domuni's first steps as a 'start-up'. How did it evolve?

Domuni is a company, and must be better than a company, while remaining a company. We receive no subsidies from anyone. We have been searching for an economic model that will enable Christianity to endure in an era of collapsing institutions. The 'material cause', as the Thomists or Aristotelians would say, is essential. If we are not financially stable, no one will help us

We have adopted a quality-focused, low-cost model. As a liberation theologian, I believe that it is the poor who drive history forward. When you pool everyone's limited resources, abundance is created. Domuni's development demonstrates that this approach works. This year, we signed agreements with several universities, including the Université Notre-Dame in Haiti, the Université de l'Assomption in the Congo, the Université d'Uélé in the DRC, Tangaza University in Kenya, the Université Saint Dominique de l'Afrique de l'Ouest in Burkina Faso, the Université Saint-Joseph in Beirut and the Université del Norte Santo Tomas in Argentina.

By pooling our resources, we have just created a business school offering four highly varied master's degrees, as well as master's degrees in economics and development and economic ethics. I'm amazed that the lecturers have offered to teach their courses for free. The teachers offered their courses without any compensation –I find it remarkable. They made the initial contribution, and later they'll handle the grading. It's a supportive and intelligent world we're living in. It's working, and it's very encouraging.

Let's move on to Teilhard. Why did you propose - under the guidance of Friar Jean-Michel Maldamé[180] - a course on Teilhard?

I first heard about Teilhard from my grandmother and mother, who had also read his work. Teilhard illuminated all my studies, starting with my agronomy studies. I started reading his work in my final year of high school and continued in the preparatory class, finishing the complete works at the beginning of my second year as an agronomy student. While working at the Vendargues cooperative cellar near Montpellier, I was in charge of vinification and spent my free time on the cellar's roof with Teilhard's books, which I annotated scrupulously. The harvest from the whole valley came together beneath me, and I could see the pickers and the tractors bringing the skips towards me in the distance. I was a focal point. There was an analogy with what I was reading –it was cosmic. I should mention that the wine that year was excellent, and I was congratulated on it.

I was a disciple of a Dominican priest who wrote his theological thesis on 'Christ in Teilhard'. He wrote it at a time when the documents were still being circulated clandestinely on mimeographed sheets. My chaplain at the École Nationale Supérieure d'Agronomie in Montpellier was Jacques Martin (there are many Jacques Martins!). He was also a doctor of law. He was a very intelligent man, but unfortunately he never wrote an article on Teilhard. I had already discovered Teilhard's work before, and I came to understand it better through the structured lectures he gave to students. Everyone has a special mentor.

The essence of Teilhard's vision lies in his emphasis on meaning. We tend to discuss the meaning of life in an intellectual sense –it makes sense. For Teilhard, and for Christians, it is much more than that. There is meaning because there is direction. The world is inhabited by a story that is going somewhere. And why is that? Because of a promise.

Similarly, Teilhard discovered this in evolution. The universe is in motion; it has been evolving for billions of years. We can discern

---

[180] Jean-Michel Maldamé, OP, has a university education in both philosophy and science (mathematics and philosophy of science), and holds a doctorate in theology. He has given many courses at Domuni.

a sense of direction towards greater complexity, organisation and consciousness; it is moving towards unity. This is scientifically proven. Teilhard would have been delighted to witness what we now call globalisation. The globalisation he experienced was that of world wars and colonisation. Nevertheless, in his excellent book *Écrits du temps de la guerre*, he observes an increase in collective awareness. Humanity must take control of its own destiny. This is clearly evident today in the context of ecological challenges, pandemics and economic issues.

Teilhard is a scientist, a visionary and a mystic in the truest sense. He is also a poet. He creates beautiful imagery and writes remarkably well. Despite the terrible circumstances he had to live through, his vision is very biblical, historical and incarnate, full of hope and faith. He wrote in the trenches during the war of 1914. He was then virtually exiled because his ideas were too revolutionary to be accepted. He was banned from teaching and publishing, but nothing could stop him from communicating what he saw.

He is a prophet. He has inspired me greatly, and I can tell you that, as you have probably experienced, nothing beautiful or great comes without suffering, injustice, obstacles and jealousy. Teilhard is an intellectual genius and, in my opinion, a great saint. Some saints are not canonised until centuries after their death, and this will be the case with Teilhard.

He was a great contemplative, and his vision of the mystery of Christ was ultimately very traditional, closely aligning with that of the Greek Fathers. He lived before the Second Vatican Council, a difficult time for scientists who were grounded in their faith.

After that, I was a student chaplain and introduced them to Teilhard's ideas. If you want to be a believer, it's important to have something credible and thought-provoking to hold onto. I helped the students to imagine the world in which they live: an evolving, historical world that comes from far away and goes far beyond us, dragging us along with it. I call this mysticism: feeling part of a movement. It's not just moralism, telling people what to do. It's more about showing the meaning of life and joy. I used a text by Teilhard that I thought summed up his thinking very well: 'My phenomenological perspective on the world'. The first part of the text doesn't require faith; he demonstrates the obvious evolution of this world and, therefore, its meaning and direction. I'm simplifying it slightly to summarise quickly: there have been different stages. Then he asks himself, 'How is this possible?' He introduces the idea of revelation: could it go all the way if there wasn't something attracting us? If the result didn't already exist before we got there: that's the problem of eschatology, if we can put it in theological terms: Christ has already risen, and at the same time we are moving towards him.

Domuni has been a 'noospheric adventure' for you. Where does it stand today? What is your assessment? What developments do you foresee?

We have been operating in an experimental mode, experiencing different situations and adapting to them.

I studied philosophy with Michel Henry, a phenomenologist from Montpellier who later became a Christian. He explained that action, praxis, reveals things. It is through action that we discover. This was similar to Domuni's principle.

From the outset, we decided to emphasise that Christians should have access to the intellectual aspects of the faith. In some cases, however, we have no control over this; it's done remotely, which upsets some professors because they would prefer to have an audience, even if they do correct the homework.

Passing on knowledge that used to be reserved for the few but is now accessible to all is a kind of revolution. Isn't this a matter of urgency? We can see that things are falling apart everywhere.

Another initial option was using written communication. We received a number of different opinions, with some advocating the use of videos. The technical problem with this is that videos are not suitable for people in poverty. In many places, the connection quality is not good enough. After discussing the matter with our Jesuit friends, we concluded that written communication is the most precise and fastest way of transmitting knowledge.

We have chosen the written word as our basis deliberately and philosophically. After all, we are part of the written word, alongside the Bible and all philosophical writings. Thank goodness Thomas Aquinas didn't give in to the temptation to burn his own works, despite considering them to be 'chaff'!

Other experimental choices were made, such as using the free Moodle platform. This works very well and allows for a different approach to time and space, as well as to synchronous and asynchronous learning.

You were especially well-equipped to handle the challenges posed by the pandemic!

Yes, universities were in a hurry and thought they could directly transpose classroom courses into remote synchronous streaming, which is not so simple.

Lockdowns led to a 100% increase in activity. Another growth factor has been the grants we have awarded, which have allowed certain students to register on our platform and access a whole range of courses for free. Right now, we're experiencing a significant change. As I mentioned earlier, we are receiving requests from underprivileged universities in countries such as Argentina, Haiti, Lebanon, Congo, Kenya and Burkina Faso, which means that we are beginning to work directly with our students, as well as through partner universities. We are in the process of changing our model and passing through a 'critical threshold', which is also reminiscent of Teilhard's ideas.

A considerable amount of voluntary work is required, which demands a high level of motivation. Domuni is an experience that fosters enthusiasm. It's a way of experiencing globalisation that would have fascinated Teilhard.

Contents

A snapshot of Domuni in 2023 9
   The university context 16
   Domuni, a theology school 23

The genesis of the institution (1997-2005) 43
   Protohistory 43
   Brother Hervé Ponsot, O.P. 52
   Brother Michel Van Aerde 63
   Should it be an association or a company? 75
   Institutional and academic development 78
   Financing, both ordinary and extraordinary 83

Taking off (2005-2020) 91
   Marie Monnet, Dominican lawyer and theologian 91
   Ecclesiastical recognition 93
   Summer university 98
   New languages and international development 101
   Civil recognition 103
   Some international events 120

Distance can rhyme with chance 135
   For a theology of distance 135
   Diversification and autonomy 146
   Facilitating the network: face-to-face visits 148
   Colombia and Peru, spring 2022 157
   Argentina, the UNSTA, December 2023 169
   An archipiélago of academic institutions 175

Appendices 187

DOMUNI-PRESS
publishing house of DOMUNI UNIVERSITAS

« The book grows with the reader »

Domuni Universitas

Domuni Universitas was founded in 1999 by French Dominicans. It offers Bachelor, Master and Doctorate degrees by distance learning, as well as "à la carte" (stand-alone) courses and certificates in philosophy, theology, religious sciences, and social sciences. It welcomes several thousand students on its teaching platform, which operates in five languages: French, English, Spanish, Italian, and Arabic. The platform is accompanied by more than three hundred professors and tutors. Anchored in the Order of Preachers, Domuni Universitas benefits from its centuries-old tradition of study and research. Innovative in many ways, Domuni consists of an international network that offers courses to students worldwide.

To find out more about Domuni:
www.domuni.eu

The Publishing House

Domuni-Press disseminates research and publishes works in the academic fields of interest of Domuni Universitas: theology, philosophy, spirituality, history, religions, law and social sciences. Domuni-Press is part of a lively research community located at the heart of the Dominican network. Domuni-Press aims to bring readers closer to their texts by making it possible, via the help of today's digital technology, to have immediate access to them, while ensuring a quality paperback edition. Each work is published in both forms. The key word is simplicity. The subjects are approached with a clear editorial line: academic quality, accessible to all, with the aim of spreading the richness of Christian thought. Six collections are available: theology, philosophy, spirituality, Bible, history, law and social sciences. Domuni-Press has its own online bookshop: www.domunipress.fr. Its books are also available on its main distance selling website: Amazon, Fnac.com, and in more than 900 bookshops and sales outlets around the world.

To find out more about the publishing house:
www.domunipress.fr

EXTRACT FROM THE CATALOGUE

Jean-François ARNOUX,
    Et le désert refleurira.

Sabine GINALHAC,
    Désir d'enfant. L'éclairage inattendu des récits bibliques.

Pierrette FUZAT,
    Un nom au bout de la nuit. Le combat de Jacob.

Patrice SABATER,
    La terre en Palestine/Israël.

Marie MONNET,
    Emmanuel Levinas. La relation à l'autre.

Apollinaire KIVYAMUNDA,
    Maurice Zundel, une biographie spirituelle.

Juliette BORDES,
    Viens Colombe. Saint Jean de la Croix.

Joseph MARTY,
    Christianisme et Cinéma.

Michel VAN AERDE,
    Le père retrouvé

Monique-Lise COHEN, Marie-Thérèse DESOUCHE,
    Emmanuel Levinas et la pensée de l'infini.

Claire REGGIO,
    Le christianisme des premiers siècles.

Ameer JAJE,
    Diaconesses. Les femmes dans l'Église syriaque.

Jean-Paul COUJOU (sous la direction de),
    L'État et le pouvoir.

Françoise DUBOST,
    L'Évangile des animaux.

Markus JOST,
    La Bible à l'école d'Ignace de Loyola et de Menno Simons.

Paul TAVARDON, ocso,
   Trappistes en terre sainte. Des moines au cœur de la géopolitique. Latroun, 1890-1946 (T.1).

Paul TAVARDON, ocso,
   Trappistes en terre sainte. Des moines au cœur de la géopolitique. Latroun, 1946-1991 (T.2).

Marie MONNET (sous la direction de),
   La source théologique du droit.

Nilson Léal DE SA,
   La vie fraternelle.

Apollinaire KIVYAMUNDA,
   Maurice Zundel. La relation à Dieu.

Lara LOYE,
   Fraternités.

Bernadette ESCAFFRE,
   Vocations. Quand Dieu appelle.

Raphaël HAAS,
   Pleine conscience. Bouddhisme et christianisme en dialogue.

Augustin WILIWOLI,
   Axel Honneth. Lutter pour la reconnaissance.

Louis FROUART,
   Pascal. Cœur, Corps, Esprit.

Emmanuel BOISSIEU,
   Platon. Une manière de vivre.

Emmanuel BOISSIEU,
   Kant. Une philosophie de la liberté.

Marie MONNET,
   Dieu migrant.

Thérèse HEBBELINCK,
   L'Église catholique et les juifs (T.1 et T.2).

Béatrice PAPASOGLOU,
   Qu'est-ce que l'homme ?

Augustin WILIWOLI SIBILONI op,
   Ce que les philosophes disent du vivre-ensemble.

François MENAGER,
    Yves Bonnefoy, poète et philosophe.

Nicole AWAIS,
    L'art d'enseigner le fait religieux.

Thérèse M. ANDREVON,
    Une théologie à la frontière (T.1 et T2).

Michel VAN AERDE,
    Venez vous reposer. Antidotes spirituels au burn-out.

Agnès GODEFROY,
    Bien vieillir, dans les pas d'Abraham.

Olivier BELLEIL,
    Résolution des conflits dans l'Église primitive.

Anton MILH op & Stephan VAN ERP,
    Identité et visibilité. Conflits de générations chez les Dominicains.

Denis LABOURE,
    Astrologie et religion au Moyen Âge.

Jorel FRANÇOIS,
    Voltaire, philosophe de la religion.

Augustin WILIWOLI SIBILONI op,
    La reconnaissance. Réparer les blessures.

Jean Baptiste ZEKE,
    Loi naturelle et post-humanisme.

Emmanuel BOISSIEU,
    Paul Ricœur. Un inconditionnel de l'amour.

Ameer JAJE,
    Le chiisme. Clés historiques et théologiques.

Jean-René PEGGARY,
    L'aube d'une pensée américaine. L'individu chez H. D. Thoreau.

Jean-François ARNOUX,
    Comme un feu dévorant. Flammèches d'une lecture incarnée de la Bible.

Olivier BELLEIL,
    L'autre dans l'islam coranique.

Sœur Agnès DE LA CROIX,
    Miroir juif des évangiles.

Jean-Michel COSSE,
    Au centre de l'âme.

Jean-Paul BALDAZZA,
    Antoine. Un saint d'Orient et d'Occident.

Ameer JAJE,
    Marie dans l'islam.

Olivier PERRU,
    Le corps malade.

Jesmond MICALLEF,
    Trinitarian Ontology.

Abel TOE,
    Pauvreté et développement au Burkina Faso.

Jude Thaddeus MBI AKEM,
    Le développement en Afrique.

Claude LICHTERT,
    Lire la Bible ensemble.

Jorel FRANÇOIS,
    Voltaire, philosophe contre le fanatisme.

Bruno CALLEBAUT,
    Les Évangiles. Leurs origines, leurs exégèses.

Claude LICHTERT,
    La parole pour sortir de soi. Dieu et les humains aujourd'hui : parcours biblique.

Heriberto CABRERA REYES,
    Effondrement, apocalypse ou renaissance ? Théologie en temps de crise.

Patrick MONJOU,
    Comment prêcher à la fin du Moyen Âge ? (T. 1 et T. 2).

Robert PLÉTY,
    À la découverte du Rabbi de Nazareth (T. 1).

Robert PLÉTY,
    À la rencontre du Rabbi de Nazareth (T. 2).

Jules KATSURANA,
    Guide pour la Prévention de la violence sexiste.

Jacques FOURNIER,
    La Trinité, mystère d'amour.

Louis D'HÉROUVILLE,
    Marie-Madeleine, femme pascale.

Olivier PERRU,
    Martin-Stanislas Gillet (1875-1951). La peur de l'effort intellectuel.

Paul-Marcel LEMAIRE,
    Vivre l'Évangile.

John Jack LYNCH,
    Judith, Sarah and Esther. Jewish heroines.

Paul NYAGA,
    Moral Consistency with Lonergan's Thought.

François FAURE,
    Emmanuel Mounier : La personne est son engagement (T. 1).

François FAURE,
    Emmanuel Mounier : Montrer, sans démontrer (T. 2).

Olivier-Thomas VENARD, Gregory TATUM,
    Conversations sur Paul. « Supportez-vous les uns les autres ».

Isaac MUTELO,
    Muslim Organisations in South Africa. Political Role Post-1948.

Stephen Musisi KASOZI,
    Issues of Constitutionalism. A case study of Uganda.

Pierre Dalin DOMERSON,
    La gestion des biens de l'Église. Enjeu Pastoral.

Philippe ANDRÈS,
    Notre-Dame de Rocamadour. Du Moyen Âge à nos jours.

Oliver BARRETT,
    Ecological Crisis. In Catholic Social Teaching.

Augustin WILIWOLI SIBILONI,
    Négociation pacifique des conflits sociaux.

Alfred DIBAN KI,
    Ubuntu et vie chrétienne.

Claude VALENTIN,
> *99 Questions sur l'Humanitaire.*

Philippe MONTOISY,
> *Le chien militaire et la Première Guerre mondiale.*

Alice NEPVEU-BARRIEUX,
> *La marine dans l'Ancien Testament. Représentations et enjeux.*

Marie MONNET,
> *En chemin.*

Christophe-Marie, O.P. MOGHA NGAMANAPO MUDAKA,
> *Quelle crise d'éducation ? Des slogans segmentés à l'hyperconscience de la liberté holistique.*

Caroline FERRER,
> *Saint Jérôme. La représentation dans la collection Fesch en Corse.*

Munguci D. ETRIGA,
> *Kwasi Wiredu. Thoughts. Conference proceeding from Tangaza University.*

Isaac MUTELO,
> *Human Rights in Southern Africa. Theory and Practice.*

Marc MITRI,
> *Le christ-médecin. La divinisation de l'homme comme guérison selon Grégoire de Nysse.*

Manuel RIVERO,
> *Progresser dans la vérité. Père Marie-Joseph Lagrange, dominicain.*

Bruno CALLEBAUT,
> *Les évangiles au carrefour des exégèses.*

Michel VAN AERDE,
> *Domuni, Une aventure collective. 1998 – 2023.*

Didier PETERS,
> *La chaise et l'électron. Analyse de la pensée d'Alfred North Whitehead.*

Augustin WILIWOLI,
> *Justice sociale : Nouveaux enjeux.*

Claude VALENTIN,
> *De Lascaux à l'intelligence artificielle. Histoire de la culture.*

Michel VAN AERDE,
> *Domuni, una aventura colectiva. 1998 – 2023.*

www.ingramcontent.com/pod-product-compliance
Lightning Source LLC
Chambersburg PA
CBHW061939220426
43662CB00012B/1962